Charles R. Swindoll

MULTNOMAH PRESS

PORTLAND, OREGON 97266

Other books by Charles R. Swindoll
You and Your Child
For Those Who Hurt
Starting Over
Hand Me Another Brick
Killing Giants, Pulling Thorns
Standing Out
Three Steps Forward, Two Steps Back
Improving Your Serve
Make Up Your Mind
Strengthening Your Grip
Encourage Me
Growing Strong in the Seasons of Life
Dropping Your Guard

Unless otherwise identified, Scripture references in this volume are from the *New American Standard Bible*, copyright The Lockman Foundation 1960, 1961, 1962, 1963, 1968, 1971, 1972, 1973, 1975, 1977. Used by permission.

Scripture quotations marked NIV are taken from the *New International Version*, copyright 1978 by the New York International Bible Society. Used by permission of Zondervan Bible Publishers.

Scripture quotations marked *Living Bible* are from *The Living Bible*, copyright 1971 by Tyndale House Publishers, Wheaton, Illinois. Used by permission.

Book photography and design by Paul Lewis.

STRIKE THE ORIGINAL MATCH
© 1980 by Charles R. Swindoll, Inc.
Published by Multnomah Press
Portland, Oregon 97266
Printed in the United States of America

Library of Congress Cataloging in Publication Data

Swindoll, Charles R
  Strike the original match.

  1. Marriage.   I. Title.
BV835.S95   248.4   80-15639
ISBN 0-930014-36-7
ISBN 0-930014-37-5 (pbk.)

84 85 86 87 88 89 90 91 — 16 15 14 13 12 11 10 9 8

IN MEMORY OF

my mother Lovell
who went home in 1971

and my father Earl
who joined her in 1980.

Together, they now enjoy eternity
with our Lord.

CONTENTS

A Study Guide for this book is available through
Multnomah Press.

INTRODUCTION

While I write these words, strange voices and unusual sounds echo through our house. A layer of dry-wall dust has settled on most every piece of furniture. The carpet is ripped up and rolled back in two rooms, exposing a cold, bare concrete slab and ugly foam rubber padding. Naked wires dangle where light fixtures once burned brightly, and the downstairs shower is out of commission – and will be until the tile work is finished. The doorbell doesn't work nor does the patio light out back. For almost a week I've seriously considered hanging a sign out front:

DISASTER AREA – ENTER AT YOUR OWN RISK.

Our kids have begun to request maps to help them find their rooms. Not even the dog is sure where she sleeps any more. Nor am I!

You guessed it. We're remodeling. Our house is getting an extensive face-lift. In fact, it's more like radical surgery. If you've gone through the process, you don't need any further explanation. If you haven't, you wouldn't believe it if I told you.

There are four things nobody can deny who has endured remodeling:

1. It takes longer than you planned.
2. It costs more than you figured.
3. It is messier than you anticipated.
4. It requires greater determination than you expected.

The only thing that keeps the Swindolls halfway sane these days is hope. All six of us force ourselves to see the finished dream in our minds . . . and, until then, hang tough. "Some day (we keep repeating) it will all be done." *Tell me it's true!*

A marriage is a lot like our house. While new it sparkles. Fresh smells, fun surprises, and new discoveries make each day snap, crackle, and pop. Sure, there's work to be done, but the newness takes away the hassle. As time passes, however, things change. Slowly, almost imperceptibly, the grit of responsibility mixed with the grind of routine starts to take its toll. Who hasn't experienced it?

Bills come due. Weeds sprout. Doors squeak and sag. Windows stick. Paint peels. Roofs leak. Faucets drip. Drains clog. Floors lose their luster. The fun 'n' games silently erode into relentless, demanding, irritating tasks. The dreams fade into the misty memories of "the way we were," introducing us to nightmarish and fearful feelings of "the way it is."

That warm, passionate fire that once cast its spell upon us is obviously dying down. Thoughts and words once foreign to us now reside in our heads and tumble out of our mouths. Suddenly we realize we're faced with a decision: move out or stay and remodel. Walk away from the embers or rekindle the fire. Too often the first choice is considered the romantic resolve. The honeymoon is over . . . dreams lie broken and scattered . . . there is nothing left of the relationship that once was. The duet has become a duel. The smiles and laughter that once made coming home sheer ecstasy have turned into lonely stares and sighs of disappointment. The magic is gone. Nothing is left in its place except cold mental mirrors reflecting yesterday's sunshine that today has been eclipsed.

Years ago, I read somewhere that getting married is like buying an album of music. You really like one side of the record, but you have to take the flip side with it. Right now, however, you feel like all you've got is the hole in the middle! Gone are those romantic strings with their magnetic melo-

dies of a lingering embrace, kisses of reassurance, and quiet 11
evenings of treasured pleasure. Instead of caring-and-listen-
ing communication, you get busy signals . . . and you do not
know how to repair the lines.

Enter the advice of others:

*"Look, you don't have to keep torturing yourself.
Bail out! Life's too short to spend it in a losing battle.
You've given it your best shot and it hasn't worked—so,
give it up. Or the least you can do is try an exciting
affair. Get a little fun back into your life. There are
lots of available and attractive lovers with no strings
attached. We're living in the 1980s, not the 20s! Things
are a lot different now. Love today means 'never
having to say you're sorry,' not 'I'm stuck with this
creep the rest of my life.' And marriage is okay for those
who are too insecure to cut it on their own. But you're
not the type. Why stay in that miserable cage? You are
free! Walk away and never look back—everybody's
doing it."*

This is no exaggeration. And every year the assault is
greater. Heavy verbal artillery pounds away at weak marriages
and the fragile strings that hold many homes together. With
relentless and merciless regularity, those screaming shells
land with telling blows, leaving the bruised and bloody victims with the choice of digging in or dropping out.

You don't need to be told which option many married
couples are choosing today. Chances are good you yourself
have entertained the thought of selling out. It's certainly
easier to bail out than to work through. At least it seems so at
the present time. Remember the four? It takes a lot of time.
It's costly. It's just plain messy and painful. It's tough. Toughest thing you can imagine! Furthermore, when we're surrounded by so many "authorities" who say that starting a new
fire is so much more exciting than stoking an old one, it's not
only tempting, it's downright appealing.

But deep down inside you, there's something tugging at
you, urging you to stay at it, to pay the price, to stir up what's
there rather than kick aside the charred remains of what was
once so enjoyable, so fulfilling. That "something" dare not be

12 ignored! It may very well be the voice of God quietly yet forcefully reminding you of those words:

> *... with love, I take you,*
> *...for better, for worse*
> *... till death do us part.*

That's what this book is all about. It offers a strong challenge. I mean it when I say it's not for babies. It's really designed for you who are willing to get down to business and let the Bible strike the original match as you and your partner glean God's timeless truth to help you rekindle that fire. For sure, He will see you through the whole process.

Essentially, this is a biblical book on marriage. You've already found that bookstores—non-Christian and Christian alike—have several shelves bulging with books on marriage. Many offer clear logic and current ideas, some interesting psychology, good philosophy, and even colorful pictures surrounded with amazing stories, fascinating experiences, life-changing testimonies, and moving devotional thoughts. Most are written by qualified people, many of them Christians—good books by good authors who believe in the Good Book—but as I read them, I keep asking, "Where are the Scriptures that support your point?" Or, "That sounds right, but is that a biblical principle or a personal one?"

This volume attempts to fill that gap. I assure you, everything of significant importance will be drawn from the Bible, God's original blueprint for married couples to follow. But this doesn't mean I'm going to preach at you. You will soon discover that these things I share are realistic, believable, positive, nontechnical, and free from perfectionistic demands. Read that sentence again. As I write about marriage, I promise to filter everything through those five checkpoints.

Along with numerous references to the Bible, I frequently mention my own marriage. Not because it's perfect, but because it's the only marriage I really know in depth. Since we began our partnership together on June 18, 1955, Cynthia and I have worked through some extremely difficult times. We have been determined to take God at His Word and do those things which He says *will* work! For almost a quarter of a century (!) we have learned how to survive and flex, grow and

forgive, using the very same principles I mention in this book. **13**
They are too good, too valuable, too necessary to keep to
ourselves.

With the addition of four active children (two teenagers, two
soon to be), we've put these things to the acid test. *They work.*
If they didn't, I would never waste your time or mine. Ours is a
home occupied by six sinners, plain and simple. We live with
all the built-in hazards that could lead to fractured relationships and collapsed bridges of communication. Life in this
Southern California zoo is life in the raw, friends and neighbors. If a marriage can stay strong out here, those principles
being used need to be passed around. Our only claim is God's
abounding grace that enables us to change in some area
almost every day so that harmony might prevail as we keep rekindling the fire.

If we can do it, anybody can. And that includes you. Admit-
tedly, it's lengthy, costly, messy, and hard work. But it's not
impossible. When you consider the alternative, it's well worth
all the time and effort involved.

Charles R. Swindoll
Fullerton, California

1

LET'S CONSULT THE ARCHITECT

The American family is in trouble. Bad trouble. Marriages are hurting, even Christian marriages. Strangely, the happily married couple seems an oddity in our times. This is true even among those we once admired.

An executive from one of my publishers visited me several months ago. En route to the West Coast, he made several overnight stops, hoping to make contact with potential authors. When we met for dinner, he was obviously more somber than I had ever seen him. As I probed he responded,

"Chuck, on my way out here I made six stops, each in a major metropolitan area of our nation. At each place I either heard about or dealt with influential, once-respected Christian statesmen—solid evangelicals, men committed to the truths of Scripture—who have left their wives."

Shocked, I asked if these individuals seemed broken . . . if they felt they had done everything possible to hold their homes together. I will never forget his answer.

"Broken? No way! As a matter of fact, most men left their wives for another woman . . . and they are still engaged in the Christian ministry as if nothing ever happened."

16   It is this new dimension of an old problem that has prompted me, more than anything else, to write a book on marriage. Unhappy marriages, domestic conflicts, and spiraling divorce rates have always been among us. For years people have been asking, "Is it realistic and right to enforce a 50-year contract on a 20-year-old couple?" Wives and husbands alike have walked away from one another for decades. A "permanent marriage bond" has never been a unanimous American opinion. Especially among non-Christian people. The sign that hung in the Hollywood jewelry store window for several months some time ago didn't even make front-page news in the *Los Angeles Times:*

WE RENT WEDDING RINGS.

So what's the big deal . . . *in the world system.*

There is a new wrinkle, however, that troubles me in all this. This temporary commitment to marriage is now being embraced by many Christians. Frankly, I'm a little surprised when I see a happily married, non-Christian couple. I'll tell you, they're pulling off an amazing feat! On the sheer force of human ingenuity and man-made determination, they are hanging in there. But the Christian couple?

Listen, we have the power and presence of the living Lord available to us, the prayer support of others in the family of God, the inner-working of the Holy Spirit, plus the divinely-inspired handbook of instruction on marriage and the home . . . not to mention pastoral instruction week after week, marriage and family conferences, and helpful books and tapes on the subject. Our cup is abundantly full and running over.

In spite of all those resources, Christian husbands and wives are walking away. Willfully. Openly. Unashamedly. In many cases, free of any twinge of guilt or the slightest fear of God. I'll tell you, we have come upon an unusual era. It is difficult enough to exist in the smog of troubled and broken marriages among the unsaved world . . . but now that the same syndrome is floating into the Christian family, it's time to get involved in some effort that can turn the tide.

We need to blow the dust off God's original blueprint for marriage and the home. Our great need is to hear what He has to say to His people about His design. After all, marriage is His invention. It's obvious that He understands it best, since He holds the patent on it. As the Master Architect, the Lord is the most qualified authority, so we seek His counsel first and foremost. Let's hear what He has to say about His invention.

A "Good" Reason for a Relationship

It is in the second chapter of Genesis that we find the first detailed reference to the first man and woman. Theologians refer to such scriptures as a "passage of primary reference." If we expect to grasp God's viewpoint of the marriage relationship, an understanding of Genesis 2:18-25 is crucial.

> Then the Lord God said, "It is not good for the man to be alone; I will make him a helper suitable for him."
>
> And out of the ground the Lord God formed every beast of the field and every bird of the sky, and brought them to the man to see what he would call them; and whatever the man called a living creature, that was its name.
>
> And the man gave names to all the cattle, and to the birds of the sky, and to every beast of the field, but for Adam there was not found a helper suitable for him.
>
> So the Lord God caused a deep sleep to fall upon the man, and he slept; then He took one of his ribs, and closed up the flesh at that place.
>
> And the Lord God fashioned into a woman the rib which He had taken from the man, and brought her to the man.
>
> And the man said, "This is now bone of my bones, and flesh of my flesh; she shall be called Woman, because she was taken out of Man."
>
> For this cause a man shall leave his father and his mother, and shall cleave to his wife; and they shall become one flesh.
>
> And the man and his wife were both naked and were not ashamed.

This event occurred on the sixth day of the creative week. God performed miracle after miracle, day after day. On four distinct occasions He passed His approval on His creation.

> . . . God saw that it was good (1:12).
> . . . God saw that it was good (1:18).

18

>*. . . God saw that it was good* (1:21).
>*. . . God saw all that He had made, and behold,*
>   *it was very good* (1:31).

But what do you notice about God's statement regarding Adam in Genesis 2:18?

>*. . . it is not good . . . .*

This is the first time in all the Bible that God says something is *not* good. What is *not* good? God declares it isn't good for man to be alone. This isn't just a passing comment. In the original Hebrew, the language in which the Old Testament was written, the negative is most emphatic; therefore, it appears first in the phrase. Literally it says, "Not good, is man's aloneness. . . ." God, the Creator, saw man, His creature, in an isolated, alone-condition. He announced that Adam's solitary state was not good. God cared about Adam's "aloneness."

I will never forget performing a wedding for a couple who had been engaged for about two years—quite a long while when you're in love. The groom was as anxious as any man I've ever seen. During my preliminary, introductory comments in the ceremony, I chose to read this verse—Genesis 2:18. No sooner had I explained the emphatic statement, "not good, is man's aloneness," than the nervous groom sounded forth a stage whisper you could hear in a little theater off Broadway: *"AMEN!"* Who knows? Maybe Adam did the same. Being all alone, living an isolated, lonely life is hard to bear, something troubled partners tend to forget as they contemplate divorce.

Aloneness Answered

But the Creator did more than declare a problem. He announced the solution:

>*"I will make him a helper suitable for him."*

We'll look at these verses more in depth in Chapter 2. But for the moment, notice the first title God gave the woman: *helper*. Our English word doesn't sound very important. In fact, my latest copy of Webster's New Collegiate Dictionary sets forth this definition:

helper *n.*: one that helps; *esp.*: a relatively unskilled worker who assists a skilled worker, usu. by manual labor[1]

Wow, in this day of aggressive feminists, them's fightin words! The Hebrew, however, is much more meaningful. It conveys the idea of someone who "assists another to reach complete fulfillment." It is used elsewhere in the Old Testament when referring to someone coming to rescue another. God's answer to man's lonely existence was a woman . . . one who would be there to be a vital part of his finding fulfillment, one to rescue him.

And if that isn't vivid enough, God adds that the one He would bring alongside Adam would be "suitable for him." Literally, "corresponding to" him. She would provide those missing pieces from the puzzle of his life. She would complete him as a qualified, corresponding partner. It is a beautiful picture of a dignified, necessary role filled by one whom God would make and bring alongside the man. In God's original design the plan was to have each partner distinct and unique, needing each other and therefore finding fulfillment with each other.

God Gives Away the Bride

After predicting, God performed. He made the woman from man's rib. Listen to the account:

> So the Lord God caused a deep sleep to fall upon the man, and he slept; then He took one of his ribs, and closed up the flesh at that place.

> And the Lord God fashioned into a woman the rib which He had taken from the man, and brought her to the man.

What a fabulous scene! The term "fashioned" means "to build, to rebuild so as to cause to flourish." God rebuilt that rib so uniquely that the thing came to life. It "flourished" into a lovely creature . . . Adam's God-given partner.

It then says that God "brought her to the man." After which, Adam exclaimed, "This is it!" *(Living Bible).* Today the groom would say, "Right on! All right, that's the one!" Adam realized she had been made by God, given to him by God, and

20   designed especially for his needs. Small wonder we read of his excitement.

This is a tender, touching scene. You and your wife would do well to relive it and put it into today's language and needs. Mutual respect must somehow be restored. It is in that context that love flourishes. In God's original blueprint we find the woman needed by the man, significant to the man, and even honored alongside the man. We also see the man finding completeness and fulfillment, neither of which were possible without the woman. Transparently, he exclaims "This is it!" As if to say. "She's the one!" Openly, he declares his gratitude.

I am especially impressed with the fact that God *personally* brought that particular person to Adam. What a thought! Your marriage will turn a vital corner when you realize that it is the Lord who personally prepared your mate for you. No doubt you have different temperaments, different interests, different perspectives, tastes, abilities, personalities, and moods. It is these differences that add variety and color to your marriage.

I was well over ten years into our marriage before I became aware of the value of this principle, that is, being grateful for the differences between my wife and me. For over a decade I resented it, I now admit to my embarrassment. I was often irritated that she didn't view things exactly as I viewed them . . . that she frequently represented another side of an issue . . . you know, another opinion than mine. It wasn't that she was argumentative (I often was!) but only expressive of her honest feelings. She approached a situation differently than I, she saw other shades of meaning, she had other feelings. I took that as a lack of submission and told her so. Time and again we locked horns until finally God showed me from this "passage of primary reference" that my wife was different because *he had made her different.* She was all the more valuable to me because of those differences. She was not designed to be my echo, a little vanilla shadow curled up in a corner awaiting my next order. She was designed by God to be my counterpart, a necessary and needed individual to help me become all God wanted me to be.

Four "Musts" for Marriages 21

Now, back to these last two verses in Genesis 2.

For this cause a man shall leave his father and his mother, and shall cleave to his wife; and they shall become one flesh.
And the man and his wife were both naked and were not ashamed.

Take a few extra seconds to read those words again—slowly and thoughtfully, preferably aloud. You'll observe an absence of quotation marks—indicating these words were probably not a part of the original dialogue between God and Adam. Observe also the mention of father and mother. Obviously, these verses have a much broader scope than Adam and Eve, for the original couple had neither father nor mother. I suggest that many years later God gave Moses (the one who wrote Genesis) these thoughts to record as guidelines for all marriages throughout time. They stand as the earliest definitive statement ever made regarding marriage.

Having meditated on these words for an extended period of time, I want to offer four foundational guidelines for a meaningful marriage. Each term is related to a portion of these two verses. You might want to put them in the margin of your Bible.

. . . a man shall leave his father and mother	SEVERANCE
. . . and shall cleave to his wife	PERMANENCE
. . . and they shall become one flesh	UNITY
. . . and the man and his wife were both naked and were not ashamed.	INTIMACY

Without wanting to oversimplify marital conflicts and complications, I can say that in most every difficulty I've dealt with, one or more of these guidelines were either ignored or violated. They are basic to domestic harmony. I state that unequivocally so you will take them seriously. Chances are good that if you do so, you will begin to find the right combination that opens the vault leading to some answers you've been looking for. Because they are so important, I will postpone our probing into each until the next chapter.

22   Before doing so, however, let me warn you against approaching these guidelines in a mechanical manner. In other words, try not to view these things as "four steps to absolute marital harmony," like an airtight, magic formula. They must be blended with *wisdom, understanding,* and *knowledge.* Without these three vital ingredients, all attempts at rekindling the fire that once kept your marriage warm will fail.

Changing the Floor Plan

Turn to Proverbs 24:3-4. Take the time to ponder these words Solomon wrote centuries ago:

> *By wisdom a house is built,*
> *And by understanding it is established;*
> *And by knowledge the rooms are filled*
> *With all precious and pleasant riches.*

The writer offers dependable counsel regarding the home. He is not referring to material things, such as matching drapes and carpet, a two-car garage, or a new sofa. No, these verses say the real answer does not rest in what we possess but in what we are. Your marriage will not be restored because you buy the right things but because you become the right one. These two verses don't even mention people. A home is built by wisdom . . . its structure is established by understanding . . . its rooms are enriched by knowledge.

Look at the verbs: built, established, filled. They are words that suggest action, progress, change, aren't they? The first word, "built," comes from the Hebrew term meaning "to restore."It's the idea of rebuilding something so that it flourishes. It's the same word we just read in Genesis 2 where God took Adam's rib from his chest and "rebuilt" the bony substance into Eve. The point Solomon is making is clear. Any home can be restored, rebuilt. It is never too late. But it isn't automatic. Wisdom is needed. We'll think more about that in a moment.

"Established" means "to set in order, to place in an erect or upright position" something that is falling or twisted. Understanding is needed for this.

Third, each room is "filled," meaning "overflowing," and the idea includes fulfillment, abundant satisfaction. Knowledge makes that happen. The "precious and pleasant riches" mentioned here have nothing to do with tangible possessions—but rather the essential things that make life full and meaningful. Things like positive attitudes, good relationships, pleasant memories, mutual respect, depth of character. The things that cannot be destroyed even though your home may burn to the ground.

I first taught these truths about the essentials for life in our church in Fullerton and I tried to make the point clear with an illustration. I suggested that everyone imagine driving home from church that Sunday afternoon, turning the corner that leads to their street—then suddenly realizing as they turned into their driveway that their house had burned down to the foundation. Nothing remained except a naked brick fireplace and the concrete slab covered with smoldering chunks of wood. I added that even though such a calamity might occur, none of the "precious and pleasant riches" would have been destroyed. You cannot burn memories or relationships. Fire can't destroy character or attitudes.

Tape recordings were made of those messages on marriage. They now reach around the world. Three years later I received a letter from a woman who had heard the tape with that illustration. Listen to her words:

> Dear Pastor Swindoll:
> Two years ago I was hosting a weekly Bible study in our home. We had selected a series of your tapes to study, and while listening, one of your messages sunk deep into my heart . . . .
> You were speaking on storing our treasures in heaven. You asked the question, "What would you do if you drove into your driveway and found a pile of ashes?"
> That question really got me, as I had a houseful of three generations of antiques which I had restored. These "things" were my roots, reminding me of loving memories of grandparents.
> Well, six months later I drove in my driveway and found our two-story home in a pile of glowing red ashes. I really praised the Lord for so lovingly preparing me six months prior by hearing your message on tape . . . .
> I instantly knew that I hadn't really lost a thing . . . .

24   Remarkable. And so true. No tragedy can destroy the things that make a marriage strong.

You see, a major mistake is being made in our day. Couples are working overtime to purchase things, to add more gadgets and conveniences and elaborate appointments to their houses. But those things don't satisfy. They soon fade and fail.

The Three Vital Ingredients

God says we need only three essential ingredients to restore our marriage and make it flourish again. They are:

Wisdom. Seeing with discernment. It's having a broad perspective. The term stresses accuracy, the ability to sense that which is beneath the surface. Wisdom doesn't skate.

Understanding. Responding with insight. Establishing your marriage calls for this ingredient. As I view something with discernment (from God's perspective), I am better equipped to respond with insight, not to take it personally or feel the need to fight back.

Knowledge. Learning with perception. It includes having a teachable spirit, a willingness to hear, a desire to discover. Knowledge includes taking the time and going to the trouble to learn. Growing, healthy mates are in constant pursuit of the truth.

Let's put these two verses back together into an amplified paraphrase.

> *By means of wisdom—the skill to see with discernment, maintaining a broad yet accurate view of life—a house is rebuilt, restored so that those within it don't simply exist, they flourish, they reach their full potential. By means of understanding—the ability to respond with insight, gaining a full awareness of situations that results in an insightful response rather than a surface reaction—one brings order and an upright condition back to a marriage and home.*
> *By means of knowledge—the willingness to learn with perception, becoming acquainted with the facts and grasping their significance so that ignorance is*

dispelled and truth is continually pursued—one causes each life to be filled to overflowing with riches that can never be destroyed, like memories, positive attitudes, mutual respect, and a depth of character.

Now you see why I warned you against becoming "mechanical" as if operating with a magic-formula mind-set. Now you see why I wanted to come to terms with these essentials before going into the four guidelines in Genesis 2:24-25. To implement each guideline will require wisdom, understanding, and knowledge. You simply cannot crank out four quick little principles and suddenly expect your marriage to blossom.

It Can't Be Done!

No doubt, you're asking *how?* How can I gain wisdom and understanding and knowledge? The answer is not a list of dos and don'ts, believe me. Nor can you get them from some book or seminar or by traveling to some location in the world where these things are dispensed. The answer, again, is in the Bible. Turn to Proverbs 2:6.

For the Lord gives wisdom;
From His mouth come knowledge and understanding.

A companion verse is Psalm 127:1:

Unless the Lord builds the house,
They labor in vain who build it;
Unless the Lord guards the city,
The watchman keeps awake in vain.

The Lord alone can give you these skills and abilities. You can't do it on your own. Working independently of Him will accomplish zero. Frustration and futility will haunt you if you try to do it in your own strength. Remember, it is the *Lord* who gives these gifts. Unless the *Lord* pulls it off, you labor in vain. This means you need to be a Christian . . . and you need to turn to Him regularly. I'll spell out some practical hints in the pages that follow; but, at the bottom line, only the Lord can give you these three essential ingredients. Remember, marriage is *His* invention. He holds the patent.

The time to start is *now*. Remember Adam? God stepped in and said, "Not good!" Face the music. Declare your need. Start today.

26   The method to follow is *God's*. No need to run down to the city library and check out five or six books. They will disagree and you'll be confused. God's method is direct and to the point. Follow His instructions.

The person to change is *you*. Not your mate. Not your circumstance. With wisdom, understanding, and knowledge, you can experience a whole new frame of mind. You can actually be fulfilled in spite of less-than-ideal circumstances. The person to focus on all through this book is you.

Charlie Shedd was right. "Marriage . . . is not so much finding the right person as it is *being* the right person."[2] I want to talk about that in the next chapter. Better take a deep breath before you dig into it, however. It may hurt. Normally, you have to blast before you can build.

If you're willing, then start with me at ground level. Let's repair the foundation.

---

[1]*Webster's New Collegiate Dictionary*, s.v. "helper," © 1980 by G. & C. Merriam Co.
[2]Charles W. Shedd, *Letters to Karen* (Nashville: Abingdon Press, 1965), p. 13.

2

LET'S REPAIR THE FOUNDATION

It was on one of those television talk shows several months ago. The guest was an actor, well-known for his romantic roles on film. Predictably, he was asked, "What makes a great lover?" I am confident everyone watching the show (myself included) expected the standard macho-playboy response. To the surprise of the host and the audience, his answer must have raised eyebrows all across America. It went something like this:

> "A great lover is someone who can satisfy one woman all her life long . . . and who can be satisfied by one woman all his life long. A great lover is not someone who goes from woman to woman to woman. Any dog can do that."

Wow! May his tribe increase. Unfortunately, our actor friend is outnumbered by many more so-called authorities on the subject of marriage. A war is raging, in fact. It is a shouting war waged in the press and movies, on TV screens and lecture platforms, among college students and angry women's liberationists, and in today's reading material. Hardly a week passes without our hearing that marriage represses and degrades women. Believing this to be true, universities from Maine to California have now added to the

28   curriculum courses offering information on alternatives to marriage, declaring that the age-old family concepts are in transition, soon to be replaced with domestic options for the nuclear age.

Is the war real or theoretical? Has the bombardment been effective? According to a survey of student opinion conducted by Daniel Yankelovich, Inc., in 1971, the number of students who believed that marriage is obsolete was increasing substantially. The results showed an alarming 24 percent. By May, 1971, it had leaped to 34 percent, one out of every three![1] And that survey, remember, will be a decade old in 1981. No, the war on marriage is certainly not theoretical. And even if you are genuinely committed to your mate, you cannot keep from suffering somewhat from the fallout and flak that splatters across our society.

In the previous chapter, we learned from Genesis 2 that the God who created man and woman also invented the way they could live in harmony with each another. Likewise, we gleaned from Proverbs 24:3-4 three truths to help us find fulfillment in our marriage: wisdom, understanding, and knowledge. Without these at work in our relationship, we will lack the protection from enemy attack as our own marriage will be weakened and ultimately lose its fire.

Let's reread Genesis 2:24-25, that "passage of primary reference," and dig deeper into those early guidelines the Lord gave Adam and Eve. Remember, now, they are for *all* marriages, not just the first one. This is verified by the fact that Jesus, many centuries later, returned to the Genesis 2 account when answering a question regarding divorce (Matthew 19:4-5). Paul did the same when he addressed the subject of marriage in Ephesians 5:22-33. These guidelines are timeless and as relevant and dependable today as the first day God gave them. Although ancient, familiar, and reliable, they are nevertheless continually ignored.

Severance

The first directive God declared was:

"For this cause a man shall leave his father and his mother . . . ."

In order for the new relationship between bride and groom to 29
flourish and their home to begin correctly, the cord must be
cut with the parents. This does not mean abandoning our
parents or ignoring or mistreating or cutting off all contact
with them. To "leave father and mother" means to break the
parent-child bond, to sever the tight, emotionally dependent
strings that once provided security, protection, financial
assistance, and physical needs. All or any of those ties, if
brought over into a marriage, will hinder the bond of marriage from sealing. So God mentions this first, even before He
talks about "cleaving" to each other.

This is sound advice for parents to heed just as much as it is
for those getting married. Release your child! That is perhaps
the best wedding gift you can give. Ideally, verbalize your
willingness to sever those ties. I know of some parents who
actually wrote their feelings and decision on a piece of paper,
giving it to the bride and groom on the wedding day. Good
idea!

More and more I am including the parents in the wedding
ceremony, asking them to stand and publicly agree to release
their parental authority and entrust their offspring to the
new home beginning that day. This, I believe, cements the
decision and makes it permanent in everyone's mind. Newly
married couples need that freedom before they are able to give
themselves fully to one another.

Severance must permanently impact the bride and groom
as well. Leaving father and mother is a painful, difficult
decision for some. In fact, it keeps many a person from cultivating a serious relationship with the opposite sex. I smile
every time I hear the American folk song, *Billy Boy*. Maybe
you didn't learn all the lyrics, so you never discovered why
Billy Boy and his girlfriend didn't marry. When you sing,
"She's a young thing and cannot leave her mother," you get
the impression she was twelve or thirteen . . . or certainly not
over fifteen. Right? Wrong! Listen to the stanza:

How old is she, Billy Boy, Billy Boy?
How old is she, charming Billy?
Three times six and four times sev'n,
Twenty eight and elev'n,
She's a young thing and cannot leave her mother.[2]

30   Can you believe that? Billy Boy's girlfriend was 85 years old!
Makes one wonder how old her *mother* was. But all along, she
was viewed as "a young thing and cannot leave her mother."
That old folk song contains a common misconception.

Severance is basic to a healthy marriage. May I add one final
thought along this line? Your husband is your husband, not
"daddy," wife. Your wife is your wife, not "momma," husband.
No matter how many children God gives you . . . no matter
how long you may have been married, calling each other
"mother" and "daddy" can take its toll on your romantic
feelings for each other. You leave father and mother . . . you
don't marry them!

Permanence

In order for a marriage to survive the war,
each couple needs to view the commitment to each other as an
irrevocable, permanent bond. Read the verse again:

*"For this cause a man shall leave . . . and cleave
to his wife . . . ."*

Leave and cleave. Sever and bond. Loosen and secure.
Depart from and attach to. The Hebrew term, translated
"cleave" means "to glue, to cling." Moses writes of diseases
"clinging" to the body. Job mentions bones "clinging" to the
skin. Both use this same original word.

Today's problem is largely explained by the fact that couples
enter the marriage relationship believing it is terminable. "Til
death do us part" is, unfortunately, a mere verbal formality to
many who utter those words. The whole concept of establishing a permanent bond between a husband and a wife is
quickly becoming a foreign thought. More and more it is
being interpreted, "Til disagreement do us part" or "Till other
interests do us part." It was never meant to be so in God's
original match.

Cynthia and I, for several years now, have determined to
strengthen our relationship by declaring our permanent commitment to each other. This is something we took for granted
far too long. It is no longer something we assume. Periodically, through the year (especially on New Year's Day, our
anniversary, and each other's birthday), we affirm our commitment, eyeball to eyeball, stating our love and devotion to

each other. This really helps! We do not consider separation even an option, no matter how hot the disagreement—and, believe me, it gets awfully hot at times. This is all part of cleaving to each other. Regardless of the difficulty or the problem we are working through, the bond God sealed in June, 1955, is not ours to break.

During England's darkest days in the late 1930s and early 1940s, it was a pudgy, cigar-smoking, unimpressive-looking man who held the country together. While other voices were shouting, "*Surrender!*"—Sir Winston Churchill stood fast. Bombs devastated city blocks, buildings crumbled, bridges fell, but the stubborn Prime Minister refused to budge. Never once did he consider capitulating or even negotiating with the Nazis. He operated on a rather simple rule of thumb when it came to winning a war. On numerous occasions Churchill stated his philosophy in six words:

"Wars are not won by evacuations!"

Surrendering is not an option if you plan to win a war . . . or succeed in a marriage. I firmly agree with that San Francisco attorney I heard in a meeting some time ago, "There are two processes that must never be started prematurely: embalming and divorce."

Severance from dad and mom is first. Permanence between husband and wife is next. Third is . . .

Unity
Listen to these words once more:

For this cause a man shall leave his father and his mother, and shall cleave to his wife; and they shall become one flesh.

It's the last part that interests us. Becoming one flesh suggests a process, not an instant fact. Two people with different backgrounds, temperaments, habits, scars, feelings, parents, educational pursuits, gifts, and interests don't immediately leave a wedding ceremony in perfect unity. The process *begins* there, however. And it is a lifelong project requiring wisdom, understanding, and knowledge.

Unity is not to be misconstrued as uniformity. God brought Eve to Adam . . . not to be a female Adam but to be distinctly

32   unique, obviously different from him. Uniformity occurs in donut shops as bakers punch out their pastries. It happens in Detroit as long assembly lines crank out Chevys. It is essential in a Marine boot camp as young men are squeezed into the same mold. But that is not what God had in mind when He stated that the two would become one flesh.

The whole idea of mutual acceptance, giving, listening, forgiving, belonging, and direction was implied. It is two individuals willingly blending into each other's lives, desiring to share with and thereby complete the other. Read Paul's words along this line:

> Let the husband fulfill his duty to his wife,
> and likewise also the wife to her husband.
> The wife does not have authority over her own body,
> but the husband does; and likewise also the husband
> does not have authority over his own body, but the
> wife does (I Corinthians 7:3-4).

The picture is one of total unselfishness, two persons actively engaged in "fulfilling" his/her duty . . . to the partner. How rare today!

The following statements were taken from a suggested "Marriage Contract" I heard about from a friend who had read about it in some secular magazine.

> I will not give come on signals to others for sexual relations when I see that you feel threatened . . . we are separate people with our own standards and they must never be fused into one . . . I cannot make you happy or unhappy, but I can make myself happy . . . I accept my ultimate aloneness and responsibility for myself.

What a joke! I ask you, where's the unity?

Few people are able to express this concept of unity better than the late Peter Marshall. He described marital harmony this way:

> Marriage is not a federation of two sovereign states.
> It is a union—
> domestic
>   social

spiritual
  physical.

It is a fusion of two hearts—
  the union of two lives—
    the coming together of two tributaries,
  which, after being joined in marriage, will flow
in the same channel
  in the same direction . . .
carrying the same burdens of responsibility and
obligation.[3]

Rekindling your marriage fire calls for a severance from parents, a permanence in the seal, a growing unity as two become one and . . .

Intimacy

Take time to consider the order of things as God reveals these timeless guidelines. Surrounded by the security of commitment to each other, the acceptance brought on only by mutual respect and love, and an undeniable unity of purpose and goals . . . the joys of personal intimacy are not only present, they *flourish.* That explains why

. . . the man and his wife were both naked and
were not ashamed.

This guideline of intimacy is mentioned last in God's foundational list. There's a reason, though. The delights of intimacy between a husband and his wife are enjoyed because severance, permanence, and unity are obviously in operation. Remove the context of these other three foundational pillars and *whoosh!,* intimacy quickly disappears.

Before I describe how this facet of intimacy in marriage is being twisted today, let me probe deeper into Genesis 2:25. The Hebrew term translated "naked" suggests the idea "laid bare," emphasizing totally and completely naked. When the verse adds that Adam and Eve "were not ashamed," the idea from the original construction is reciprocal—they weren't ashamed "before or with one another." Amplified, the picture is they had no hidden areas, no hang-ups, no embarrassment, no fears. There was total transparency, the complete absence of self-consciousness. This gave them unrestrained

34   freedom. Emotionally as well as physically. Inwardly and outwardly.

The absence of sin allowed such unhindered ecstasy. I find it exceedingly significant that in the very next chapter of Genesis, when sin entered into their lives, Adam and Eve immediately covered up. And for the first time, they admitted an awareness of their own nakedness. Listen to Genesis 3:9-10.

> Then the Lord God called to the man, and said to him, "Where are you?"
> And he said, "I heard the sound of Thee in the garden, and I was afraid because I was naked; so I hid myself."

Why the cover-up? "I was afraid . . . so I hid myself." for the first time in *all* of time, mankind became self-conscious. Up to that point, each was so totally involved in the other (thanks to their sinless condition) it never dawned on them that they were naked. Their unguarded transparency prompted unrestrained intimacy with each other. That was exactly as God originally meant it to be.

How different today! Crippled, diseased, and blinded by the pollution of sin, people wrestle desperately to relate freely and openly. The same is true of marriage partners. Intimacy, therefore, often becomes a frustrating struggle, a strange mixture of selfishness, embarrassment, dissatisfaction, and resentment . . . with only brief glimpses of pleasure and fulfillment. Because this subject is somewhat complex, I have reserved an entire chapter in which we can come to terms with the major issues—chapter 5.

Some, of course, think an answer to sexual frustration is in having an affair or two . . . or three. The grass always looks greener, doesn't it? It certainly seems easier. Instead of cultivating and acquiring the skills of intimacy (yes, there are definite *skills* involved in lovemaking), extramarital escapades seem to offer the ecstasies of pleasure without the agonies of responsibilities.

Right? Well, you decide after reading this. My good friend, Joyce Landorf, is appreciated as an author because she tells it straight. *Tough and Tender*, one of her many bestsellers, is no exception. In that excellent chapter, "The Gentle Lover," she mentions a man she calls George, who used to work at her husband's (Dick) bank. George's recent divorce led him into the swinging scene of sexual liberation. If anybody ever looked like the most enviable California bachelor in banking, George certainly did. A beach apartment. Beauty queens in and out. No-hassle sex night after night. The guy had it made. Or did he?

Listen to the flip side.

> . . . one afternoon George came up to my husband's desk and haltingly said. "Uh, Dick, could I talk to you about something?"
>
> Then, as nearly as Dick can remember, this is what George related. "You know, Dick, I've really got it made. I'm free from the attachments of marriage. I've got this great pad at the beach and I go to bed with one sexy gal after another. I come and go as I please and I do my own thing. But something is really bothering me and I can't figure it out. Every morning as I get dressed for work I look into the mirror and I think 'What was last night's sexy little game all about? Sure the girl was good-looking. She was good in bed and she left this morning without bugging me, but is that all there is in life?' I asked myself, 'If this life style is what every guy thinks he wants, why am I so depressed? Why do I feel a cold nothingness all the time?' "
>
> He stopped, leaned closer to Dick and quietly continued. "I know the guys here think it would be fantastic to have this kind of liberated freedom but honestly, Dick, I hate this life." He sat back and paused for a few seconds and then wistfully added. "You know what I'd really like? I'd like to go home tonight, smell dinner cooking, hug my wife hello, and spend the evening telling her and showing her how much I love her. I'd like to go to bed with her and not have to prove my virility, not have to sexually perform above the call of duty, but just give her love, and go to sleep knowing she'd be there in the morning." [4]

There it is, my friend. Straight scoop from an honest guy. Intimacy, fulfilling, enjoyable, meaningful intimacy must

36   emerge from the God-ordained context of commitment and
acceptance and marital harmony. That's all part of His
arrangement. The original design cannot be improved upon,
even though the propaganda sings another tune. Dance to
that strange music, and believe me, you'll pay the piper. And
he's expensive.

> Well, there they are:
>   severance
>   permanence
>   unity
>   intimacy

Foundational guidelines upon which everything rests. And
the tools needed to construct the project?
    wisdom
        understanding
            knowledge
Being ingenious, man will fiddle around with the original
design and make changes. Erasing this, rearranging that,
taking out, adding to . . . until it scarcely resembles what the
Lord God created. And the result? Just look around. Listen to
the media. Check the courtroom. Read the latest stuff. You
won't see much resemblance.

The Christian Medical Society offers its helpful journal to
our generation. It is both relevant and insightful. Several
months ago the issue was dedicated to the problem of divorce.
Included in the publication was an article lifted from *The
Washington Post* entitled "Open Marriage . . . Broken
Marriage."

> *"Open Marriage," by George and Nena O'Neill, was
> a book for the times and it said over and over again that
> you should be honest, straight, out-front, give space, let
> the other person do their thing, communicate and if you
> wanted to have an affair, for God's sake, do be honest
> about it—don't sneak around, make excuses, call late
> in the afternoon with some cock-and-bull story about
> work. Simply pick up the phone and say, "Honey, I'll be
> a bit late tonight. I'm going to have an affair."*
> *But there were these couples I know. They were open.
> They were honest. They were having affairs. They
> were not sneaking around (applause), they were not*

lying (applause), they were being honest (whistles). They were being open. Everyone agreed that it was wonderful. The men agreed and the women agreed and I agreed and it all made you wonder. Then they split. There was something wrong. Invariably, someone couldn't take it. It has nothing to do with the head. The head understood. It was the heart; it was, you should pardon the expression, broken.

It all made you think. It made you think that maybe there are things we still don't know about men and women and maybe before we spit in the eye of tradition we ought to know what we're doing. I have some theories and one of them is that one of the ways you measure love is not with words, but with actions—with commitment, with what you are willing to give up, with what you are willing to share with no one else.[5]

Whether Richard Cohen, the one who wrote that, is a Christian or not, I cannot say. But he's got his finger on the pulse of the problem. Maybe you see yourself in the mirror of his message. Perhaps some things are becoming increasingly more clear to you. Possibly God is breaking through those years and showing you that your marriage is shaky because a poor foundation was poured.

Don't be afraid to say so. Admission of a problem is the first step toward solving it. And it's often a *giant* step. If you're willing to repair the foundation, then you shouldn't have too much difficulty choosing the bricks that will help rebuild your marriage.

[1]Lester Velie, "The War on the American Family," *Reader's Digest,* January 1973, pp. 106-110.

[2]"Billy Boy," *Folk Songs for Everyone* (New York: Remick Music Corporation, 1962), p. 54.

[3]Catherine Marshall, *A Man Called Peter* (Lincoln, Va.: Chosen Books, 1951), p. 54.

[4]Joyce Landorf, *Tough and Tender* (Old Tappan, New Jersey: Fleming H. Revell Company, 1975), pp. 132-133.

[5]Richard Cohen, "Open Marriage . . . Broken Marriage," *The Washington Post,* © 1977 and reprinted by permission.

BRICKS THAT BUILD A MARRIAGE

Four-year-old Suzie had just been told the story of "Snow White" for the first time in her life. She could hardly wait to get home from nursery school to tell her mommy. With wide-eyed excitement, she retold the fairy tale to her mother that afternoon. After relating how Prince Charming had arrived on his beautiful white horse and kissed Snow White back to life, Suzie asked loudly:

"And do you know what happened then?"

"Yes," said her mom, "they lived happily ever after."

"No," responded Suzie, with a frown, " . . . they got married."

In childlike innocence, that little nursery schooler spoke the in-depth truth without realizing it. Getting married and living happily ever after are not necessarily synonymous.

Check the stats, if you're not convinced. "The American Family" was one of the feature articles in a national periodical some time ago. It was enlightening, informative . . . and depressing. Especially the grim graph that revealed the growing divorce rate. Hang on. In 1960, there were 25 divorces for every 100 marriages in America. In 1975, the rate jumped to

40 48 divorces per 100 marriages. The article stated that at the present rate of increase, there will be 63 divorces for every 100 marriages by 1990.[1] In case you haven't a calculator handy, that's an increase of 150 percent in one generation. Happily ever after? Not quite.

We are learning that a major factor in this growing problem is that couples have departed from God's original design. His blueprint has either been changed or ignored altogether. The foundation He planned has not been poured correctly. So it isn't surprising the construction fails to pass the test of time. Repairs are costly and time-consuming . . . but that's the only way. And as the process of restoration transpires, hope and encouragement return.

Remember what we uncovered earlier from Proverbs 24:3-4?

> By wisdom a house is built,
> And by understanding it is established;
> And by knowledge the rooms are filled
> With all precious and pleasant riches.

A marriage *can* be rebuilt by "wisdom." It *can* be set in order by "understanding." It *can* actually be filled with indestructible things that no calamity can remove and no thief can steal. That takes "knowledge." I want to keep reminding you of those three ingredients, lest you think that rebuilding your house into a home is simply a brick-and-mortar proposition. A sensitive, insightful spirit, a responsive, positive attitude, a teachable, willing heart are bottom-line essentials for a marriage. Keep that on the front burner, for sure.

But there are some practical building materials God has ordered for His design. We're told about these materials—these bricks—in letters from Paul and Peter in the New Testament. (When I was preparing this chapter and realized we were going to get the counsel of Paul and Peter, I was tempted to entitle it "Peter, Paul, and Marriage.") In Ephesians 5 Paul gives us the pattern for the overall structure, the superstructure. In 1 Peter 3, Peter specifies the bricks along with the mortar to bond them together.

A Superstructure That Supports

No one can claim he has done a thoroughly biblical study of marriage without dealing with Ephesians 5:22-33. In these verses, Paul first speaks to wives (vv. 22-24) and then to husbands (vv. 25-33). In both sections there is a basic role declared and then an analogy to emphasize the significance of the role.

Wives

Paul writes:

Wives, be subject to your own husbands, as to the Lord.

For the husband is the head of the wife, as Christ also is the head of the church, He Himself being the Savior of the body.

But as the church is subject to Christ, so also the wives ought to be to their husbands in everything.

It doesn't take a Greek scholar to see that Paul gives a command, "Wives, be subject to your own husbands . . . " and then a comparison . . . "as to the Lord." For wives, the basic role is one of submission, and the analogy is "as to the Lord." As the Christian wife would respond to her Lord, so she is to do to her husband.

Husbands

Paul adds:

Husbands, love your wives, just as Christ also loved the church and gave Himself up for her;

Again, it isn't complicated. The husband's basic role is adoration . . . and the analogy is ". . . as Christ also loved the church and gave Himself up for her."

Both roles have unique patterns and both are analogous to Jesus Christ. The godly wife asks, "Lord, how can I show my love to You in the role you have called me to fill?" God answers, "My dear child, show it in your submissive heart toward your husband." The godly husband asks, "Lord, how can I be the kind of man you want me to be as a husband?" God answers, "My son, your limitless love for your wife shows the world and shows Me the kind of love you have for Me."

42 Two Questions

Tucked away within the seams of these verses are two implied yet penetrating questions each partner needs to ask. The wife must come to terms with her role and ask, "Do I love my husband enough to *live* for him?" And, equally important, the husband must come to terms with his role and ask, "Do I love my wife enough to *die* for her?" Searching questions. But they put the issues in the right perspective.

The world today doesn't talk about a husband loving his wife enough to die for her. Mention that idea on any TV talk show and listen for the razz-ma-tazz from host and audience alike. And drop the word "submission" on them if you really want to wake them up—submission of the wife, that is. Immediately, you'll be categorized as some ignorant weirdo who believes in slave chambers of torture and one who promotes chaining women in a washroom. The very idea! I mean, what thinking person today can possibly imagine squashing a woman under the heels of a man . . . or shoving her in corner, reducing her activities to changing diapers, doing dishes, checking off a grocery list, and mopping floors?

Strange, isn't it, how angry and misinformed individuals invariably envision that kind of stuff whenever submission is mentioned. Everytime I hear it I know the person simply doesn't understand the biblical teaching on submission. When placed in the right setting (wisdom, understanding, knowledge), the woman's worth is *enhanced* and her life is *enriched* by a husband who adores her. There is, in that context, fulfillment and freedom rarely experienced elsewhere on earth.

Yes, I'm realistic enough to know that there will always be some who take advantage of their roles. Husbands who crack the whip because they are "in charge" . . . wives who manipulate and maneuver, using "submissive techniques" they learned from their mothers or other women. This brings incredible pressures into a home. Like this letter I received after I spoke on marriage and the family in our church:

*This series on marriage! Oh, God! How I need it!
How we need it—Joe (not his real name) and I. If these
folks around us only knew . . . but praise God, they
don't. It's somehow easier to hide behind this facade—
to play the game our friends expect of us while the
struggle merely to "hang in" strains and stretches the
last feeble threads of the web.*

*These things Paul and Peter are proposing—I've tried
them again and again and again, but it's hard, God.
You know me and Joe. Last Sunday, we were hardly
home from church when Joe began to stoke up the
management of the home role. All week, he had been
away on business and I had maintained meals and
schedules and a certain semblance of comfort and
balance. But, now it's Mighty Joe Christian, manager
of the home, telling the kids they don't have to eat their
meat loaf, that they will take naps, that my son can't
wear his new tee-shirt, and casting a reproachful look
at me when my spirit inevitably erodes with neither
gentleness nor control. Of course, it's an effort for him,
too, to insist that the children thank me for a not-that-
great pancake dinner in the evening and not call
attention to the fact that he's helping with the dishes.
And God, only You know what it must cost this man
behind closed doors to continue to offer a gift that
is not wanted.*

*But I'm here, Lord, warts and all, and so is Joe and
the threads, though warped and worn, that have kept
these volatile energies from spinning off into parallel
orbits long ago. Can it be, Lord, that these threads can
become strands in ropes and cables, if even one of us
sells out wall-to-wall for Jesus Christ? We were so sure
of that once!*

*. . . Oh, one more thing, Lord! . . . if it's all the same,
could you start with Joe?? . . . and the meat loaf??*

Even though wrongs are committed and unfair advantages
are taken, God's overall structure still stands. What we often
need is some practical help on how to pull it off. Paul has given
us that "what." Peter gives us help with the "how." Paul explains the structure, the underlying frame. Peter shows us
the actual bricks that give the marriage color and beauty.

44
Bricks That Build

In the first nine verses of 1 Peter 3, there are practical suggestions for the wife (vv. 1-6), the husband (v. 7), and a brief wrap-up (vv. 8-9).

Take the time to read all nine verses slowly and thoughtfully.

> *In the same way, you wives, be submissive to your own husbands so that even if any of them are disobedient to the word, they may be won without a word by the behavior of their wives,*
>
> *as they observe your chaste and respectful behavior.*
>
> *And let not your adornment be merely external—braiding the hair, and wearing gold jewelry, or putting on dresses;*
>
> *but let it be the hidden person of the heart, with the imperishable quality of a gentle and quiet spirit, which is precious in the sight of God.*
>
> *For in this way in former times the holy women also, who hoped in God, used to adorn themselves, being submissive to their own husbands.*
>
> *Thus Sarah obeyed Abraham, calling him lord, and you have become her children if you do what is right without being frightened by any fear.*
>
> *You husbands likewise, live with your wives in an understanding way, as with a weaker vessel, since she is a woman; and grant her honor as a fellow-heir of the grace of life, so that your prayers may not be hindered.*
>
> *To sum up, let all be harmonious, sympathetic, brotherly, kindhearted, and humble in spirit;*
>
> *not returning evil for evil or insult for insult, but giving a blessing instead; for you were called for the very purpose that you might inherit a blessing.*

Bricks for Wives

I'm confident some of you wives are thinking, "Sure, I will be glad to live like that as long as I have the right kind of husband." But these verses are written especially to the wife who has the *wrong* kind of husband. If that's your situation these four bricks are molded just for you.

The Brick Entitled "Behavior" 45

First, God talks about your *behavior*. The scene Peter paints is a familiar one. Ornery husband, raspy response, irritable temperament. But even though the guy is tough to live with, he isn't blind! He cannot ignore the behavior of his godly wife. That's what ultimately "wins" him. And the way it happens is not through little notes pinned to his pillow or elbow nudges in church. He "observes" your behavior.

Interesting term. It is the Greek word for a careful observation, a close look, like sports fans watching an instant replay of some close call. That reminds me of what once happened during the NFL playoffs a couple years ago. Being the avid football fan I am, I have managed to infect our older son, Curt, with the same disease. He and I follow the game with fanatic interest, especially when the Dallas Cowboys are playing.

All season long (and for some wives, it's *really* long), we had watched the season run its course. The Cowboys and the Rams were slugging it out for the next playoff berth. A judgment call was made by the ref and just as the instant replay began to review the action in slow motion, Cynthia snapped on the vacuum cleaner and started in on the den where we were sitting. I couldn't believe it! Curt and I were on the edge of our chairs staring, studying the call . . . and in comes Mrs. Tidy with that suction snorkel and the sound of a cotton gin.

I shouted, "What in the world are you doing, Cynthia?" Without looking up, she said, "I'm cleaning the stadium!" Don't get me wrong. She enjoys football too . . . but after four-plus months of it, the place does begin to resemble box seats at the Rose Bowl.

It's what my son and I were doing that applies to this second verse. We were not casually glancing at the replay. We were absorbed in it, focusing full attention on it. That's what husbands ultimately do when their wives' "chaste and respectful behavior" is consistently on display. It's what one man calls, "the silent preaching of a lovely life."[2]

The Brick Labeled "Appearance"

The second "brick" that helps build a stronger marriage is the wife's *appearance*.

46

> *And let not your adornment be merely external—*
> *braiding the hair, and wearing gold jewelry, or*
> *putting on dresses;*
> *but let it be the hidden person of the heart, with the*
> *imperishable quality of a gentle and quiet spirit, which*
> *is precious in the sight of God.*

Let's focus in on the main thrust of this passage. Peter's point is clear. You are warned against *going overboard*, patching up the externals if your internals are pitifully lacking. Don't place all your emphasis on the outside . . . but, on the other hand, this doesn't mean there *shouldn't* be something on the outside worth looking at.

I've heard preachers run wild with these verses. "Braiding the hair"—you see, you mustn't braid your hair, they say. "Wearing gold jewelry"—skip the accessories, they insist. It's carnal. But the verse also mentions "putting on dresses." Funny thing, I've never heard a preacher encourage nudity . . . but if he presses his forced logic, that's next.

Listen, this passage isn't bad-mouthing cosmetics or taking shots at keeping yourself physically attractive, ladies. It's just encouraging you to *keep it in balance.* Not external only, remember. Some wives need all the help they can get! Like the old saying, "If the house needs painting, *paint it.*" Good advice for wives, too. It's a shame some have not learned the importance of keeping themselves attractive. All day long their husbands encounter fantastic women, well-dressed and appealing, and what do they see when they walk in the kitchen at 5:30 p.m.? The totaled woman.

What's the difference? The importance of appearance. A man doesn't stay interested in a wife who smells like she just got dipped in Lysol. Or runs around the house looking like an unmade bed all day. For sure, you need to be pure within . . . but don't stop when you get to the outside. There's no reason in the world a Christian woman can't look attractive just as often as possible. Whatever it takes, do it! Your appearance is a significant "brick" that helps rebuild a marriage.

The Brick Called "Attitude"

There's a third: *attitude*. Look at verse 3 and 4 again.

> And let not your adornment be merely external—
> braiding the hair, and wearing gold jewelry, or
> putting on dresses;
>   but let it be the hidden person of the heart, with the
> imperishable quality of a gentle and quiet spirit, which
> is precious in the sight of God.

The phrase, "hidden person of the heart," is a New Testament description of the wife's attitude. And what characteristic in her attitude does God consider important? He mentions specifically ". . . the imperishable quality of a gentle and quiet spirit . . . ." What a beautiful expression! God views a gentle and quiet spirit as *imperishable.* And He adds that it is "precious in the sight of God." The word "precious" is from the same Greek term Peter used earlier when referring to imperishable "faith" (1:7) and the imperishable "blood" of our Lord Jesus Christ (1:19). Wives, your attitude is *that* important. It cannot be erased or passed over or destroyed.

"But I'm not gentle and quiet. God didn't make me mousey," say some of you ladies who read this. As in the case of submission mentioned earlier in the chapter, this attitude is misunderstood by many who read it. It's not a reference to being weak or a female doormat. Actually, these are terms that speak of strength of character, strong self-control, a person of quiet elegance and dignity.

One of my wife's favorite Bible verses is hidden away in the last chapter of Proverbs. It is in a context of other verses describing the "excellent wife" (v. 10). After stating how rare and capable she is, how worthy of her husband's trust, and how respected in the eyes of others, the writer drops this additional comment:

> Strength and dignity are her clothing,
> And she smiles at the future (31:25).

It's a picture of unusual beauty. She is inwardly clothed with strength of character and confidence. She isn't shallow or loud or cheap. She's got class, we would say.

48   Being "gentle and quiet" is another way of saying "tranquil and under control." Does that sound like weakness? Those who are in control of themselves and free from panic or irritation are people of amazing strength. Small wonder the one who wrote Proverbs 31 asks,

> *An excellent wife, who can find?*

When Peter uses the term, "gentle," he has in mind genuine humility, one who does not fight against either God or others. It is an absence of struggle and contention. "Quiet" indicates "tranquility arising from within, causing no disturbance to others."[3] This kind of wife isn't churning within or restless without.

Before leaving this third character "brick," I want to add that it takes only a little while to doll up the externals (important though that may be), but cultivating "the hidden person of the heart" is a lifetime process.

This was emphasized to me in an unforgettable manner as I was driving on one of our Southern California freeways some time ago. Right in front of me that morning were a husband and wife apparently driving to work together. As he drove, she dressed! I'm not kidding. She had hopped in with everything she needed to wear . . . and she worked feverishly during that twenty-five-minute ride putting it on. Including eyelashes and earrings right down to heels and hose. The drive was the only R-rated trip I've ever made. Yep, in twenty-five minutes a woman can perform a minor miracle from the skin out . . . but her "hidden person"? Ah, that's the task of a lifetime.

The Brick Designated "Response"

We've covered three "bricks" thus far: behavior, appearance, and attitude. We need one more to complete the pattern for the wife: *response*. Verses 5 and 6 form the basis:

> *For in this way in former times the holy women also,*
> *who hoped in God, used to adorn themselves,*
> *being submissive to their own husbands.*
> *Thus Sarah obeyed Abraham, calling him lord,*
> *and you have become her children if you do what is*
> *right without being frightened by any fear.*

Before your feathers get ruffled by what this says of Sarah ("obeyed"), it will help you to realize the Greek verb means "to pay close attention to" someone. It's the idea of attending to the needs of another. A positive, helpful response is written between these lines.

Wives, please listen closely. If you are the energetic type, your tendency will be to dash all over the globe, responding to the needs of people everywhere. Clubs, classes, and courses will clamor for your time. And unless you're careful, they'll get it. If not all of it, *most* of it. Even church stuff will occupy every hour you'll give. Some of you have become far more concerned about responding to others' needs outside the home than to that one individual most important to you within the home.

I can't fathom Sarah's leaving this note pinned to their tent one evening as Abraham shuffled home from work, bone-tired and dangerously hungry:

Abe:
   Mutton pot pie in the stone oven. Gone to Torah study
with the ladies at Bethel. Took the small chariot.
Be home late. Don't worry. Be sure to give Ishmael
herbs for cough at sundown. And bathe Isaac.

Sarah

P.S. Don't forget to close all the flaps when you go
to bed. Sandstorm is coming.

Some of you think, "If I start being as responsive as you suggest, my husband will take advantage of me. He'll walk all over me. Give him an inch and he takes a mile." You need to look at the last part of verse 6 again.

. . . do what is right without being frightened
by any fear.

There's your promise. God will honor your loving and supportive response, ladies. Relax. He won't allow your mate to stomp all over your gracious response. It's a brick, remember. It's solid and strong. It hurts when you stomp on bricks.

Bricks for Husbands
                     I've been tossing some tough bricks on the wives. I warned you, ladies, remodeling is hard work. But

50   now, let's see what God says to the man of the house. It is equally potent.

> *You husbands likewise, live with your wives in an understanding way, as with a weaker vessel, since she is a woman; and grant her honor as a fellow-heir of the grace of life, so that your prayers may not be hindered.*

A First Brick

The first brick for the husband is obvious: *Live with your wife.* "Hey, I do! Come home every night. We have the same address, eat at the same table, sleep in the same bed, and even use the same bathroom." But that's not all this verse is talking about. The original term translated "live" means "to dwell down," and it suggests being closely aligned, being completely at home with. The little word "with" is a term calling for close companionship, deep-down togetherness.

Many a husband looks to the wife to maintain this. "My job's the office, her job's the home. I earn the bucks, she handles the bills. The business is mine and all its headaches. The home is hers and all those needs related to it." That may be the way you were raised, my friend, but it isn't the way God originally designed it for husbands. No way. On the front end of everything the Lord says in this verse, "living with your wife" is paramount. It is our task to lay the groundwork for domestic harmony, husbands. We are the ones who should be cultivating an in-depth partnership with our mates. We are to initiate the action, encourage the process.

Cynthia and I came across this truth many years ago. It began to haunt me that I was becoming much more passive (like my own father) in matters pertaining to the home. I was leaving more and more decisions up to her, unconsciously turning over the reins of leadership. It was *convenient,* frankly. I could always use the excuse of pressures related to the church I was serving or demands on my time from people in great need for spiritual counsel. It was also a lot *easier.* Being the hot-shot down at the church was a downhill slide in comparison to the nitty-gritty leadership of the home. It was much more glamorous, far more ego-satisfying, and certainly "more spiritual" to care for the flock as a shepherd than establish and embellish a partnership with my wife.

Then God shot a right jab to my jaw with I Timothy 3:4-5,
where He writes to pastors who are also husbands:

> *He must be one who manages his own household*
> *well, keeping his children under control with all*
> *dignity*
> *(but if a man does not know how to manage his own*
> *household, how will he take care of the church*
> *of God?);*

See the word "manage"? It's mentioned twice. It means,
literally, "to preside over, to lead," but it's much broader.
Listen to this excellent explanation:

> *A good manager knows how to put other people to*
> *work. . . . He will be careful not to neglect or destroy*
> *his wife's abilities. Rather, he will use them to the*
> *fullest. . . . He does not consider her someone to be*
> *dragged along. Rather, he thinks of her as a useful,*
> *helpful, and wonderful blessing from God. . . .*
> *A manager has an eye focused on all that is*
> *happening in his house, but he does not do everything*
> *himself. Instead, he looks at the whole picture and*
> *keeps everything under control. He knows everything*
> *that is going on, how it is operating, and only when it*
> *is necessary to do so steps in to change and to modify or*
> *in some way to help.*[4]

That really convicted me! Since making the discovery and im-
plementing some changes, I have traveled to one seminary
and Bible school after another underscoring the importance
of the home life of the minister. Not infrequently, it is the *first*
time many of the men have ever considered the vital link
between their relationship with their wives and families and
the congregations they serve.

It is absolutely imperative, men, that we fight our tendency
to be passive in matters pertaining to the home. The passive
husband continues to be one of the most common complaints
I hear from troubled homes. Men, *get with it!* Your wife will
grow in her respect for you as soon as she sees your desire to
take the leadership and management of the home.

52 *A Second Brick*

A second "brick" for husbands could be put in these words: *Know your wife.* Again, this might sound like something you are already doing. The original expression, however, will help you determine if you are. Literally, the expression means "dwell together according to knowledge." The success of your dwelling with your wife, my friend, will be in direct proportion to your knowledge of her.

Knowing your wife includes those things about her that others don't and won't know. Her deep fears and cares. Her disappointments as well as her expectations. Her scars and secrets and also her thoughts and dreams. That's *knowing* your wife. It calls for a sensitive spirit, a willingness to be involved, to listen, to communicate, to care. Husbands—if your marriage is eroding this is one of the most important issues you can give yourself to. It will do as much to heal her hurts and calm the storm as anything I could suggest. Your wife longs to be understood and to know you desire that.

A Third Brick

Finally, Peter says *honor your wife.*

> *. . . and grant her honor as a fellow-heir of the grace of life*

The term rendered "grant" means "to assign" and here the husband "assigns" her a place of honor. Interestingly, the term "honor" and the previously used word "precious" are from the same Greek root. Husband, what place have you "assigned" your wife? Maybe you really value her and appreciate her. It's quite likely you genuinely view her as a precious treasure, a person you might esteem, you honor.

Does *she* know it? Have you told her? Do you demonstrate that honor you claim to have for her? Guys like us tend to assume our wives know how much they mean to us. But there is nothing like telling her. Sometimes with well-chosen words. Other times with flowers. With small, elegant gifts. With letters we mail to them while we're away. With little notes here and there. With a meal for two at one of her favorite spots. With a surprise weekend trip where new surroundings and room service and relaxing around a pool offer undeniable proof that she is significant and worth a lot to you. On the way back home, believe me, your wife won't have as much difficulty believing that you really *want* to be close to her, to know her, to honor her.

Beginning Construction

Need a place to start? Here's how. Reserve an evening soon, preferably this week. You can stay home or take a drive or go to dinner or spend the night somewhere special. The place isn't as important as the project, but you do need to be alone so you can think and talk and respond without interruption.

1. Spend at least fifteen minutes in silence, thinking about and writing down the four things you appreciate the most about your mate. Husbands, you talk first for a change. Both listen carefully.

2. Using I Peter 3:1-7 as your guide, admit the one trait or habit you would most like to see the Lord change in your life. Declare your desire to cooperate with His changing you.

3. Before going to bed, set at least two major goals for your marriage. Pray together and ask God to make them a reality rather than simply a distant dream.

4. After both finish, give the list of four areas of appreciation to each other. Keep it and review it several times that evening and during the week that follows.

If you haven't done this for a long time (for some of you— *ever!*), it will seem awkward and maybe even a little embarrassing. Handling bricks is a skill that has to be learned, you know. But once you get the hang of it, once you get hold of authentic communication, open and unguarded sharing, no substitute will do.

Fake bricks never are as attractive or valuable as the real thing. So watch out for cheap substitutes.

---

[1] The Reporter's Notes, "Family Trends Now Taking Shape," *U.S. News & World Report,* October 27, 1975, p. 32. Material taken from the copyrighted chart, "Divorce: More and More Common."

[2] William Barclay, "The Letters of James and Peter " in *The Daily Study Bible* (Edinburgh: The Saint Andrew Press, 1976), p. 219.

[3] W. E. Vine, *An Expository Dictionary of New Testament Words,* 4 vols. (Old Tappan, New Jersey: Fleming H. Revell Company, 1940), 3:242.

[4] Jay E. Adams, *Christian Living in the Home* (Grand Rapids: Baker Book House, 1972), pp. 91-92.

4

WATCH OUT FOR CHEAP SUBSTITUTES!

We are living in a day of synthetics. Imitations, counterfeits, and artificials abound. They fit our plastic world, unfortunately.

Let's face it, we've grown accustomed to cheap substitutes. Vinyl has virtually taken the place of genuine leather. Formica looks almost like wood. Artificial flowers "bloom" year-round. Substitute foods, synthetic fabrics, man-made lakes, rocks, and trees have become so perfected they are actually preferred by many. The phony appears so real, you have to examine closely or you'll be fooled. But when you get down to the details, when you really pay attention, it is obvious why the authentic is better. And when the bottom line is drawn, the genuine is always more valuable than any substitute.

Maybe you heard about the guy who fell in love with an opera singer. He hardly knew her, since his only view of the singer was through binoculars—from the third balcony. But he was convinced he could live "happily ever after" married to a voice like that. He scarcely noticed she was considerably older than he. Nor did he care that she walked with a limp. Her mezzo-soprano voice would take them through whatever might come. After a whirlwind romance and a hurry-up ceremony, they were off for their honeymoon together.

56   She began to prepare for their first night together. As he watched, his chin dropped to his chest. She plucked out her glass eye and plopped it into a container on the nightstand. She pulled off her wig, ripped off her false eyelashes, yanked out her dentures, unstrapped her artificial leg, and smiled at him as she slipped off her glasses that hid her hearing aid. Stunned and horrified, he gasped, "For goodness sake, woman, *sing, sing, SING!*"

In this chapter we're thinking about a different set of substitutes . . . but they are nevertheless just as damaging to a marriage. In fact, more so. We're thinking about things that are put on the outside to cover up what's missing on the inside. Cheap substitutes that wives and husbands are tempted to use instead of genuine qualities that make a marriage strong and stable.

Substitutes Wives Often Use

In the same passage that gave us helpful guidelines to strengthen a marriage (I Peter 3:1-9), we find some warnings against cheap substitutes. Wives, because these verses start with you, so will I. In verses 1 through 6, there are three substitutes that wives often use. If you're ready, let's roll up our sleeves and dig in.

Scheming in Secret

The first substitute is *secret manipulation.* Listen to the first two verses, ladies:

> *In the same way, you wives, be submissive to your*
> *own husbands so that even if any of them are*
> *disobedient to the word, they may be won without*
> *a word by the behavior of their wives,*
> *as they observe your chaste and respectful behavior*
> (I Peter 3:1-2).

Because we've already examined these words rather closely, there is no reason to do that again. But it will be helpful if you will observe these verses call for a quiet spirit, a wife who is characterized by control and tranquility—in spite of a disruptive home situation kept in turmoil by a disobedient husband. God says, "Let Me handle your man. You leave the preaching to Me. What I want from you is a godly life. Remember, he won't be able to ignore your quiet, calm spirit."

But that's tough! And because it is, many wives resort to a **57** substitute for this quiet spirit. They employ a technique I will call secret manipulation.

Webster says that manipulation means "to control or play upon by unfair or insidious means, especially to one's own advantage or to serve one's own purpose." In other words, secret manipulation is an unfair, insidious technique that results in getting what one wants. When handled cleverly, a wife can substitute secret manipulation for a quiet, submissive spirit.

It's been my observation that the woman who employs this substitute is usually the one who cannot leave things in the hands of God. She finds it virtually impossible to believe that the Lord can handle her husband without her help. Therefore, she resorts to any number of manipulative techniques... like moodiness, pouting, sulking, scheming, sexual bargaining, or even lying—even though she would call it "altering the truth just a little." By manipulating her man, she hopes (ultimately) to get her own way. Unfortunately, she usually does. Manipulation works!

A classic illustration of this is Isaac's wife Rebekah. Determined to get her husband to see things her way and to pass special favors and family blessings on to Jacob (her favorite) rather than the first-born Esau, Rebekah manipulated her husband. She led a secret conspiracy and encouraged a scheme that was so effective, Jacob literally tricked his dad into the plan. Genesis 27 tells the tragic story. The deed stands as an ugly, dark splotch on Rebekah's biography.

No amount of rationalization will *ever* justify manipulation, wives. Your husband cannot be manipulated into any permanent change. You may scheme and pressurize him into surrendering to your will. If you are especially good at this, you may develop just the right technique to weaken his resistance and fall into your trap . . . but *it will not glorify God.* In doing so, you will lose more than you will gain. Manipulation weakens a marriage.

Peter's counsel is wise: "without a word." Apart from schemes. Free from manipulation. Trust in the Lord your God to handle your husband. Believe me, He can!

58   Unattractive Adornment

There is a second substitute. It is the strong temptation to substitute *external appeal for internal beauty.* I wrote a little about this in the previous chapter, but more needs to be said. Before that, however, let's read I Peter 3:3-4 once again:

> *And let not your adornment be merely external —*
> *braiding the hair, and wearing gold jewelry,*
> *or putting on dresses;*
> *but let it be the hidden person of the heart, with the*
> *imperishable quality of a gentle and quiet spirit, which*
> *is precious in the sight of God.*

Remember now, the Scripture is not saying externals are totally unimportant . . . but that externals are not as important as internals. Wives, your physical appearance is indeed significant. The warning here is that it not be your primary focus or emphasis. Being subjected to the relentless bombardment of the media, you will have difficulty keeping this proper scale of priorities. Such pressure will strongly tempt you to substitute a beautiful body, attractive clothing, and exquisite accessories for the lack of quality within. God says — "Don't do it!"

Cecil Osborne refers to the woman who possesses this overemphasis on the externals as a "narcissistic woman." She is one who . . .

> *. . . has an inordinate self-love. She is unduly*
> *preoccupied with her face, her body, and often with*
> *her own interests, which she perceives as an extension*
> *of herself. . . .*
> *A man married to a narcissistic woman is in for*
> *trouble. If the world does not continue to praise her,*
> *and if he does not cater to her infantile whims,*
> *she may develop any number of physical or emotional*
> *symptoms . . . .*
> *A narcissistic woman constantly seeks to be the*
> *center of attention. She seeks flattery and is engaged*
> *in constant battle for popularity. She is sometimes a*
> *"psychic scalp collector," flirting with men in order to*
> *prove to herself that she has not lost her attractiveness.*
> *She uses men, including her husband.*[1]

For the woman who genuinely wants to be a godly wife, my advice is to give greater attention to your inner person – those "imperishable qualities" – than to your physical attractiveness. In the long run, believe me, your husband will be much more satisfied and stimulated over your inner beauty.

Learning Rather Than Doing

Let me mention one more "cheap substitute" so common among Christian wives in our day, before addressing the husbands. It is *learning about what's right rather than doing what is right.*

Listen to Peter's counsel once again:

For in this way in former times the holy women also, who hoped in God, used to adorn themselves, being submissive to their own husbands.
Thus Sarah obeyed Abraham, calling him lord, and you have become her children if you do what is right without being frightened by any fear
(I Peter 3:5-6).

Those verses mention how modern-day wives can become "Sarah's children" (i.e., a woman like Sarah) and emulate the life style she modeled. How? Look very closely at the verses:

. . . if you do what is right . . . .

It has been my observation that a large percentage of Christian wives know more – much more – than they put into practice. And yet, they are continually interested in attending another class, taking another course, reading another book, going to another seminar . . . learning, discussing, studying, discovering more and more and more. And what results? Normally, greater guilt. Or, on the other side, an enormous backlog of theoretical data that blinds and thickens the conscience rather than spurs it into action. Learning more truth is a poor and cheap substitute for stopping and putting into action the truth already learned.

Christian wife, stop and think. Please. Think about your goals, your deep-down desires as a wife. More than likely, they are commendable, probably as pure as Sarah's in ancient days. Next, think about your role. Is it clear? Is it understood? Probably so. Now then . . . in order to carry out your goals and

60   fulfill your role, do you need to learn more or start doing what you already know is right?

Please understand, I am not against seminars and feminars, courses and clubs, books and Bible studies. But it troubles me to see the same women year after year dashing to class after class instead of concentrating full and uninterrupted attention on *doing the things they've learned.*

At the risk of being misunderstood, ladies, I plead with you! Take an honest, objective look at your marriage. In all candor, do you really need more facts, more principles, or more classes this year? How about backing off and digging in? Why not take a personal sabbatical from so many activities and concentrate your full, undivided attention on your husband and your home. For sure, some people won't understand. But on the other hand, you will reap some amazing and rewarding dividends.

I am acquainted with a wife and mother of several children. She was engaged in a hectic schedule of appointments, meetings, committees, and responsibilities. All of them were good, necessary functions and closely connected with her church or related Christian ministries. Her calendar was full as she tried to juggle the car pool, the P.T.A. and other school activities, a few trips out of town with her husband, and several evenings of entertainment each month at home. There were meals to fix, lunches to pack, shopping trips, phone calls, sewing needs, and a half dozen other demands. One day she stopped everything. I mean *everything.* She sat alone in a chair at the kitchen table and thought about herself for a change. "What in the world am I doing? Why am I involved in so much? Is *all* this essential, really necessary?"

She faced the hard fact that "the hidden person of her heart" was not a gentle, quiet spirit. She acknowledged before God that her numerous involvements were displeasing to Him (and her husband, I might add). She prayed. She openly confessed her sin of substituting activity for application. She wept aloud as all this broke into her conscious realization.

The result? She canceled every possible thing she could so the essentials might take first place for a change. Her husband was beside himself with delight. Even her children

expressed gratitude to her within a week. She told me recently 61
she soon came to realize that much of the stuff she was
"learning" was not actually being absorbed at all. She now
finds herself genuinely enthusiastic about her role, her home,
and her future.

Cheap substitutes are, nevertheless, strong-willed and per-
suasive. They're like the battery — they die hard. But by God's
power they can be cast aside. Through Him, you remove those
cheap substitutes of secret manipulation, an overemphasis
on the externals, and the tendency to hectically keep learning,
going, and running instead of simply doing what is right.

Substitutes Husbands Often Use

Now let's look at the flip side of the same
record. The zoom lens of Scripture focuses now on the husband.

You husbands likewise, live with your wives in an
understanding way, as with a weaker vessel, since
she is a woman; and grant her honor as a fellow heir
of the grace of life, so that your prayers may not be
hindered (I Peter 3:7).

From this single verse, I find three more "cheap substitutes." These are the ones men frequently use in their
marriage.

Enter Provider . . . Exit Lover

The first substitute is *providing a living*
instead of sharing a life. One of the most common miscon-
ceptions husbands have goes something like this:

"Now that I have worked hard and provided you with a nice
place, sufficient food, and the clothes you need, what more
could you ask of me?"

If the guy is a Christian and likes to support his comment
with verses of Scripture, he is sure to use I Timothy 5:8:

But if any one does not provide for his own, and
especially for those of his household, he has denied the
faith, and is worse than an unbeliever.

Enter hard-working, diligent, self-satisfied, smug husband:

62   "My wife has so much more than most, she has no reason whatever to gripe!"

But wait, husbands. Your wife married *you*, not your paycheck. Of course, it's commendable that you take care of her physical and obvious needs. If you recall, you promised to do that back when you two were married. But the tendency on our part as husbands is to substitute providing for our wives in place of sharing our personal lives with them.

Recently, I buried a 42-year-old woman from our church, a fine Christian wife and mother. Beside that fresh grave the husband leaned on my shoulder and wept loudly. He sobbed as he spoke.

"I gave her everything but myself. I gave her things . . . but I didn't give her my time, my attention, my ear to listen as she spoke."

I'm honest, it's at times like that God speaks to me as well. His words hang in my head like a heavy weight. Do they convict you, too?

Peter's counsel is clear:

> *. . . live with your wives in an understanding way . . . .*

> *. . . be considerate as you live with your wives . . . .*
(NIV)

The Greek term translated "live" suggests being "at home with." Many a wife is lonely for her husband to sense and minister to her inner spirit. To give her his attention and personal presence. She waits to be noticed, to be appreciated, to be given time to share and, in return, to hear her husband respond.

With the newspaper laid aside.

With the television off.

With the whole evening available.

Men, maybe it will help to motivate you if you face the fact that a continually absent husband is a major cause for illicit affairs among wives. And often with other men who will simply give them time and attention. Wake up, husbands! Sharing your life cannot be replaced with providing nice

things. I challenge you to set aside a block of time every day . . .   63
and at least one evening every week for your wife. You cannot
imagine the benefits until you actually start that habit.

The Intimidator

Another substitute relates to the man's
leadership. Verse 7 exhorts husbands to live with their wives
"in an understanding way, as with a weaker vessel, since she
is a woman . . . ." God's Word warns us against *demanding
instead of managing.* The male—especially the insecure
male—tends to use force and intimidation, demanding certain things of his wife. The verse clearly states that of the two,
the wife is the weaker partner. She is like a delicate vessel,
deeply in need of being understood. Rare is the husband who
spends time and thought coming to an understanding of his
wife's needs so he can provide wise management as the leader
in his home. Biblical management. Wholesome, positive,
helpful management.

One reputable authority turns to I Timothy 3:4-5 and writes
about being a good manager of one's home.

> *The husband's job is to manage his family. That is
> the best translation of the word proistemi. The idea is
> "to preside over." The picture is of one who has control
> but does not do everything by himself. As the elder is to
> be a manager of a congregation, so the husband is to be
> a manager of his home. A good manager knows how to
> get other people to do things. He knows how to spot,
> develop, and use the gifts of others. That is what a
> manager is and that is what a husband is to be.*
>
> *The husband as the head of the home is its manager.
> He is the head; the head does not do the work of the
> body. The husband is not to answer every question or
> think every thought for his wife—exactly not that.
> Rather, he is to recognize that God gave him a wife
> to be a helper. A good manager will look at his helper
> and say, "She has certain abilities. If I am going
> to manage my household well, I must see that every
> last one of those gifts is developed and put to use as
> fully as possible." He will not want to squash her
> personality; rather, he will seek to bring it to the
> fullest flower.*[2]

64 Leadership like that, husbands, is the kind few wives will have trouble following. How much better than irksome, irritating demands! I have often said that the husband who shouts and bullies his way through his marriage, screaming, "I'm the leader around here!" probably isn't. Leaders are good managers, first and foremost.

My mind returns to a middle-aged couple whose marriage flame fluctuates between lukewarm and cool. The husband is the classic intimidator—strong-willed, stubborn, lacking in tenderness, and often angry. Those qualities apparently have not hurt his business. He is successful and respected by his competitors. In fact, in recent months the business has expanded . . . doubled in the last three years. Down at the office his forceful style is somewhere between awesome and fearful. People jump when he speaks. And his decisions and demands are not up for discussion. He is the boss, no doubt about it. But when he comes home, things are not the same. And he cannot handle it. He has left his wife more than once.

It's not that his wife is rebellious. Nor is she unwilling to allow him the leadership of the home. It's his forceful style—his lack of proper management—that has undercut his role as the leader. He has a *partnership* with his wife, but he is unwilling to cultivate the give-and-take such a relationship requires. He brings home the "Listen, I'm the boss!" complex, and resentment is the result. The man makes demands of his spouse that are both unwise and unfair. Among them are bizarre sexual fantasies he expects her to participate in which make her feel like a cheap prostitute in a brothel. The intimidator-type husband, by the way, usually has trouble cultivating a meaningful romance with his wife. He lacks the tenderness and care that deeply satisfying intimacy requires.

Husband, don't ignore this counsel! You may be the hotshot, fearful, decisive, awesome boss at the office, but God says you are to be a good manager, and an understanding partner at home. Intimidation will not help you cultivate a godly, healthy marriage.

The Great Smother-Up

There's one more substitute worth our time, men. It emerges from the last part of verse 7:

. . . and grant her honor as a fellow heir of the grace of life. . . .

It's what I would call substituting *smothering instead of honoring*. Loving and respecting your wife is one thing, but smothering her is another! Giving her a place of honor is both biblical and commendable, but placing her on a shelf, protecting and pampering her (for whatever reason) is neither. She is your wife, not an invalid. Not an untouchable, easily breakable china doll. Capable and competent wives need to be appreciated, for sure. But not idolized.

There's another side to smothering. It often stems from jealousy, which Solomon once said is "cruel as the grave." How true!

I once married a couple whose marriage soon suffered from the straight-jacket of smothering jealousy. The new bride and groom weren't in their home a week before he announced, "There will be no secrets between us—ever! Our marriage will have no closed doors, nothing hidden!" That morning he removed every door in the house except those that led outside. Yes, the bedroom doors, the bathroom door, the kitchen door. *Every door was gone.* No secrets! That's not honoring, it's smothering. It's ruining an intimate relationship that will flow under normal conditions. Jealous, neurotic smothering is a far cry from genuine respect and honor.

A Final Checklist

How can a husband or wife tell if he or she is using substitutes? Look at the next two verses in I Peter 3:

To sum up, let all be harmonious, sympathetic, brotherly, kindhearted, and humble in spirit;
not returning evil for evil, or insult for insult, but giving a blessing instead; for you were called for the very purpose that you might inherit a blessing.

That's an inspired checklist from God. Substitutes disrupt harmony. If there is irritation and disharmony, you are probably substituting. Substituting stops the flow of sympathy; resentment builds up in its place. Kindness ceases and hurts begin. Humility is replaced with selfishness. Insults occur as arguments increase. Ultimately, instead of building

66   up each other, an erosion in the marriage transpires as cheap substitutes finally take their toll.

In my ministry I have married hundreds of couples. But on only two or three occasions do I recall the couple coming back to me and admitting their failure to keep the marriage together. One happens to be the first wedding I ever performed. I confess I was shocked to hear it failed because the bride and groom had so much going for them.

She was a ten-talent gal who was an absolutely beautiful woman, inside and out. Well-educated, widely traveled, and deeply committed to Christ. She had a splendid position as a nurse. He was a medical doctor, having graduated at the top of his class. He planned to do his residency in the Midwest, so they wished to be married prior to the move. He was also a Christian, genuinely interested in spiritual things.

I lost track of them for almost four years. One day my phone rang. I remembered her voice immediately. She asked if we could talk that afternoon. As I met her at the door of my study, I saw a woman who looked fifteen years older. Through tears she poured out her story. The pressure began to build shortly after they arrived for his residency. He worked inhuman hours . . . and finally became dependent on drugs to continue. He saw less and less of her. Lonely, angry, and confused, she became promiscuous. Both began to fake it. Neither was willing to tell the whole truth. He worked all night, she worked all day. Month after miserable month. Arguments led to stormy fights. The cheap substitutes wore thin. Their lives were marked by spiritual compromise, gross immorality, and a growing disillusionment with life in general. Separation led to divorce.

I'll never forget her words. "As I look back, it all started when we were not honest with each other . . . when we failed to come clean and admit our needs. We substituted being phony for being real."

Here was the choice couple—models of beautiful, wholesome and healthy young Americans—with everything going for them: career, intelligence, money, happiness, and mutual love. But cheap substitutes replaced the treasured, authentic ingredients so vital in a marriage. Ecstasy turned to agony.

Your life may not be as dramatic as that, my friend, but you know exactly where you are right now. Having read this chapter, you have all the information you need to know and deal with your present condition. Reject those cheap substitutes! Stop tolerating them any longer! Come to terms with your life and your marriage now. Do some serious thinking about *yourself,* for a change. Not your mate. Be honest enough to tell the truth so God can direct you back to His original plan. In doing so He will also help you understand why your honeymoon dreams may have turned into a daily nightmare.

---

[1] Cecil Osborne, *The Art of Understanding Your Mate* (Grand Rapids: Zondervan Publishing House, 1970), pp. 201, 202, 203.

[2] Jay E. Adams, *Christian Living in the Home* (Grand Rapids: Baker Book House, 1972), pp. 76-77.

5

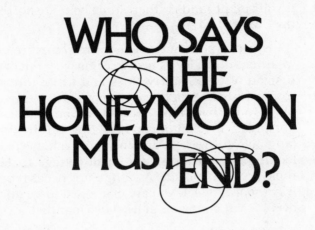

WHO SAYS THE HONEYMOON MUST END?

A harmonious marriage requires the continual destruction of myths. As fast as Hollywood can crank 'em out, married couples need to be ready to assault and destroy those fantasies!

A major myth of marriage is that it is a blissful, easy-going, relaxing cloud that floats from one restful day to the next. The guy who dreamed that one up should be *shot at dawn.*

On the contrary, a marriage that works requires a constant willingness to surrender rights, incredible unselfishness, and the ability to flex. To get this point across, let's play "let's pretend."

Pretend for the next couple of minutes that you and your mate have planned a trip to Hawaii for your mid-February honeymoon. You anticipate a warm, lazy surf, a sun-drenched beach outside your spacious hotel honeymoon suite, and lovely evenings under a clear, star-filled sky and that romantic Honolulu moon. Your expectations heighten as you board that luxurious 747 (first class, of course) and start to wing your way west.

But something strange happens in the air. Somehow the cockpit crew gets their signals crossed—and before you know

70   it your plane lands rather clumsily in the northern section of the Swiss Alps.

Instead of sunshine and a warm ocean breeze, it's subzero weather and an icy blast of freezing wind out of the northeast. Instead of clear, starry skies and white sands washed by a tropical surf, it's eight feet of snow, low clouds, the promise of more snow that night. Everywhere you look, it's bright white. For miles. Instead of good ole' English, they speak another language entirely . . . and instead of a honeymoon suite overlooking the Pacific, it's a small cottage tucked away on a rocky, rugged hillside. And the plane needs repair so you can't leave soon. In fact, you are marooned there until the freeze is over . . . which means at least two months!

Immediately you and your starry-eyed sweetie are forced to make a decision. You can adapt yourselves to the new environment—buy some winter clothes, rent ski gear, throw a few logs in the quaint old fireplace, and flex— or you can refuse to change. You can wear swimming trunks and a bikini, walk around barefoot, refuse to learn a few words of the language, and sit grim-faced in a cold, snow-covered cabin staring out the window as the snow falls.

It's really up to you.

If you flex, you can turn a tremendous disappointment into an absolutely delightful and memorable experience. Cozy evenings around a crackling fire. Fun times on the slopes. Breathtaking sights high up in the Alps. Wow! Sounds fabulous!

But if you choose to stay with "Plan A," you're in for a bitter, resentful, ugly, uncomfortable marathon of misery. Amazing! The Alps are more beautiful than Hawaii ever will be— especially in February—but for those who stubbornly resist change, *no way.*

Now, back to reality. All of us who are married anticipated a fun-in-the-sun Hawaiian delight . . . but to our surprise, it soon became evident that our marriage would be different than we expected. Welcome to the Alps! And to make matters worse, there was no flight back at the end of winter. The need? It's obvious. I've been saying it all through this book. Change. And I mean *drastic* change! The alternative is dis-

aster. And you don't need to be told that many a couple has
opted for that.

Listen, friend. Rekindling and preserving our marriage fire *demands* that we continually adjust, constantly adapt. If not, I promise you an end to the honeymoon almost before it begins. But let's be positive. Let's talk about how to keep the honeymoon from ending.

A New Name for the Honeymoon

For starters, we need to redefine "honey- moon." You're not going to like my suggestion: *adjustment period.* How unromantic can you get? I mean, who wants to say, "We went to Hawaii for our adjustment period." (Sounds like a quick trip to the chiropractor's office.)

But wait a minute. That's exactly what it is! It's the begin- ning of a whole new life style. Sure, the honeymoon does include that initial burst of physical intimacy, that period of passionate ecstasy between the wedding ceremony and the return to life's responsibilities. And it is exceedingly im- portant that such an acquaintance be as free as possible from an abrupt letdown. But basically, it is the first acquaintance with reality that both partners have in their relationship. If a couple begins this adjustment period with all four feet firmly fixed on reality, it's doubtful that they will suffer many sudden disappointments.

A Honeymoon That Never Ended

But lest I sound like an unromantic zombie that walks around in neutral when it comes to the intimate side of marriage, allow me the rest of the chapter to set the record straight. There is no reason any Christian couple needs to think that enjoying each other physically is a tem- porary, brief experience limited to a couple of weeks in Hawaii—or the Alps! If I understand correctly the things God says in His Word about marital intimacy, He never intended the sexual pleasures of marriage to end. Never. The Bible certainly implies that. Let me show you what I mean. It may surprise you.

In Chapter 2 we looked closely into Genesis 2:24-25. Once again, here's what that passage says:

72
*For this cause a man shall leave his father and
his mother, and shall cleave to his wife; and they shall
become one flesh.*

*And the man and his wife were both naked and were
not ashamed.*

You may recall the meaning of the Hebrew term translated
"naked." It is "laid bare." Nothing hidden. The absence of
self-consciousness. The original couple had maximum freedom with each other. They were unhindered emotionally,
allowing them to be uninhibited physically. That is why the
Lord reports that they were "not ashamed." The intimate joys
of the marriage bed were continually fulfilling to both Adam
and Eve. Without restraint. Without shame.

That is exactly as God would have it. Now, there is no word
here (or later) where things began to deteriorate between
them. Their intimacy apparently did not cool off nor did their
love life wane. When God struck the original match, there was
a blessed, enjoyable warmth that continued throughout that
union.

There are reasons their "honeymoon" never ended. The
same reasons can lead to a similar experience today, all things
being equal. It is incorrect to assume that original design was
unique, a one-time-only relationship God created. No, it was a
pattern for others to follow.

Biblical Principles of Marital Intimacy

Actually, there are certain biblical princi-
ples regarding marital intimacy that remain constant to this
very day. Unfortunately, those principles have long since been
bypassed or ignored. Let's blow the dust away and rediscover
them one by one.

I find a total of five principles in Scripture that will help
counteract sexual deterioration between husband and wife.
All five are supported in the Scriptures. And all five have to do
with a more meaningful, intimate relationship between
married partners, not just two people living together.

Intimacy: It Is "Very Good"

*Intimacy in marriage was created in in-
nocence and declared "very good."* Let's go back to Genesis
1:27-31:

And God created man in His own image, in the image
of God He created him; male and female He created
them.
And God blessed them; and God said to them,
"Be fruitful and multiply, and fill the earth, and
subdue it; and rule over the fish of the sea and over the
birds of the sky, and over every living thing that moves
on the earth."
Then God said, "Behold, I have given you every plant
yielding seed that is on the surface of all the earth,
and every tree which has fruit yielding seed; it shall
be food for you;
and to every beast of the earth and to every bird of
the sky and to every thing that moves on the earth
which has life, I have given every green plant for
food"; and it was so.
And God saw all that He had made, and behold,
it was very good.

Take careful note of those last two words: "very good."
Including what? Everything. And that includes, of course,
the sexual delights of marriage. God personally and caringly
created the human body so that it might be stimulated,
aroused, and able to enjoy to the fullest, in marriage, the
complete expression of sexual delight.

I begin here because this is basic. Thinking correctly about
marital intimacy lays the groundwork for enjoying it fully.
A fulfilling experience in bed begins with right thinking in the
head, quite frankly. God says it is "very good"–and so
should we.

Many years ago I taught a women's Bible class in a metropolitan city. Those who attended were clear-thinking, sharp,
"with it" ladies who genuinely desired to know their Bibles
and grow up spiritually. I'll never forget, however, how many
of them looked upon sex in their marriage as something
between a grim duty and a downright dirty experience! As I
taught on marriage, I used this (and related passages) in
Genesis. I recall how many were amazed to discover that
marital sex was created by God in innocence and viewed by
Him as "very good." One distraught and confused middle-
aged woman saw me after the class and commented that she

74   had always been convinced that "sex is part of the curse." Wrong!

Let's learn a lesson from Peter's experience in Acts 10. Let's realize that what God has cleansed we should no longer consider unholy. Now, I should add that sinful mankind has certainly twisted and polluted sex. There is every conceivable sexual perversion one can imagine, all of which are disgusting. But these are not to be confused with God's creation. Marital intimacy was, by His original design, to be enjoyed by married partners without guilt or without restraint. Note the way the Bible puts it in Hebrews 13:4.

> Let marriage be held in honor among all, and let
> the marriage bed be undefiled; for fornicators and
> adulterers God will judge.

This assures us that God views the marriage bed (another way of referring to marital intimacy) as "undefiled"–something He holds "in honor." You'll rekindle and preserve your marriage fire if you keep in mind that marital intimacy was created by God *prior to* the fall . . . and that He sees it as an undefiled, honorable part of your relationship with your mate.

Intimacy: It Is For Pleasure

There is a second biblical principle that will help keep your "honeymoon" from ending. Here is it:

Intimacy in marriage was created for personal pleasure, not just for procreation.

The fifth chapter of Proverbs is a picturesque chapter of warning. It shoots straight. Beginning on a negative note, Proverbs 5 talks first about defilement of the marriage relationship before it closes with a positive word about harmony and pleasure between husband and wife.

Listen first to the negative:

My son, give attention to my wisdom,
   Incline your ear to my understanding;
That you may observe discretion,
   And your lips may reserve knowledge.
For the lips of an adulteress drip honey,
   And smoother than oil is her speech;
But in the end she is bitter as wormwood,

Sharp as a two-edged sword.
Her feet go down to death,
Her steps lay hold of Sheol (vv. 1-5).

He goes on to describe the adulteress' feet as symbolic of the hellish life style she has adopted. If you go her way, he warns, you will wind up just like her. "Stay away!" shouts the man of wisdom.

But Solomon also adds some positive and encouraging words to his counsel. These words describe the refreshing harmony and physical pleasure God has designed for married partners to experience. The Living Bible says it well:

Drink from your own well, my son—be faithful and
true to your wife. Why should you beget children with
women of the street? Why share your children with
those outside your home? Let your manhood be
a blessing; rejoice in the wife of your youth. Let her
charms and tender embrace satisfy you. Let her love
alone fill you with delight.

All right!

If you ever had the mistaken notion that God was some sort of puritanical prude, this will certainly help dispel that idea! No, He desires that our marriages provide us with ecstatic sexual delights, exhilarating and pleasurable to the maximum.

And in case you missed it, the passage veritably extols intimate lovemaking, the joys of unrestrained, guilt-free physical delight.

Not infrequently have I counseled with couples (especially wives) who entertain the mistaken idea that once the children are born, sex has served its purpose. You know, sort of a "functional" mentality. How wrong! God's plan for intimacy between married partners is much broader than a biological necessity.

In another book by Solomon, we find similar words of marital love. The wife in this passage is looking upon her husband's body and is expressing her pleasure in his appearance.

"My beloved one is tanned and handsome, better than ten thousand others! His head is purest gold, and he has wavy, raven hair. His eyes are like doves beside the water brooks, deep and quiet. His cheeks are like sweetly scented beds of spices. His lips are perfumed lilies, his breath like myrrh. His arms are round bars of gold set with topaz; his body is bright ivory encrusted with jewels. His legs are as pillars of marble set in sockets of finest gold, like cedars of Lebanon; none can rival him" (Song of Solomon 5:10-15, The Living Bible).

Wow! Wives, if you said that to your husband tonight, *no telling what could happen!*

And there's the other side of the coin as the husband views his wife:

"How beautiful your tripping feet, O queenly maiden. Your rounded thighs are like jewels, the work of the most skilled of craftsmen. Your navel is lovely as a goblet filled with wine. Your waist is like a heap of wheat set about with lilies. Your two breasts are like two fawns, yes, lovely twins. Your neck is stately as an ivory tower, your eyes as limpid pools in Heshbon by the gate of Bath-rabbim. Your nose is shapely like the tower of Lebanon overlooking Damascus.

"As Mount Carmel crowns the mountains, so your hair is your crown. The king is held captive in your queenly tresses.

"Oh, how delightful you are; how pleasant, O love, for utter delight! You are tall and slim like a palm tree, and your breasts are like its clusters of dates. I said, I will climb up into the palm tree and take hold of its branches. Now may your breasts be like grape clusters, and the scent of your breath like apples, and your kisses as exciting as the best of wine, smooth and sweet, causing the lips of those who are asleep to speak" (Song of Solomon 7:1-9, The Living Bible).

Now that man knew how to say it! We husbands can learn a lot from this. Our wives love to hear such things said so creatively. We would do well to cultivate the ability of verbalizing our admiration.

There can be no question about it, marital intimacy is for sheer pleasure, not just for enlarging the family.

Intimacy: It Is Within Marriage

A third principle about intimacy is written between the lines of I Corinthians 7:1-2. Let's read the verses before declaring the principle:

Now concerning the things about which you wrote, it is good for a man not to touch a woman.
But because of immoralities, let each man have his own wife, and let each woman have her own husband.

Intimacy in marriage is planned for the husband-wife relationship only.

Throughout Scripture, God makes it clear that intimacy is to be enjoyed by married partners. In our world of coed dorms, wife-swapping, swingers' clubs, and unisex, this principle sounds both irrelevant and stupid. But it is true. God designed us emotionally so that sex outside of marriage is not nearly as fulfilling or enjoyable as within that secure bond.

Tragic damages occur when God's standard is violated. Let me share just one for the sake of clarification.

A great deal of my counseling time is invested in the lives of couples planning to get married. During the three premarital counseling sessions, I probe deeply into their relationship. We discuss their lives from several perspectives: spiritually, emotionally, financially, socially, and sexually. It is not uncommon for those I plan to marry to have been intimately involved with each other. I require that this be stopped if such has been the case. Before we proceed I have each one promise me that from that day on (until they are married) they will sustain restraint and self-control in their relationship.

Here's why. If promiscuity is not completely stopped for a period of time before marriage, then after marriage a strange reversal in their roles occurs. The young bride marries with disapointment over the violation done against her by her fiancé. She soon becomes dominant and aggressive, taking the role of leadership from her husband because of a mixture of resentment and anger. And the man? Well, he feels guilty, disappointed with himself, and ultimately becomes passive.

78 She takes charge (and hates it) while he backs off (and feels miserable). All because their intimate relationship was incorrectly set in motion before marriage.

Of the hundreds of unhappy couples I have counseled who finally admitted to premarital promiscuity, I can hardly recall an exception to this strange pattern. A Christian psychologist friend of mine told me that the number one problem he deals with in his busy practice is the passive male.

So many men today find it difficult (impossible?) to take the proper role of authority in their home. I wonder how much of it stems from aggressive yet immoral, illicit involvements that were maintained during courtship days . . . and now they are suffering reverse consequences.

A number of years ago, a young man knocked very hard on the door of my study. I opened the door and found him weeping. It looked as though he either had a tragic accident or lost a close friend. I had never seen him before.

"My wife and I have had a terrible, terrible argument," he sobbed.

He looked very young, so I asked, "How long have you been married?"

"One month," he replied.

"Tell me what happened."

He told how he and his bride were involved in premarital intimacy for more than two years before their wedding.

"It had become a habitual part of our relationship, and it was fairly harmonious," he said. "We thought this would be the least of our problems when we married."

But within one month after their marriage, he and his new bride experienced tremendous frustration to the point where she terribly resented his touching her. He even resented her role as she made advances toward him at times.

"As I talk with you about it," he said with sobs of remorse and sorrow, "I could not believe, even six months ago, that I could ever face a problem in this area. As a matter of fact, I'm impotent."

If you want your "honeymoon" not to end, start your marriage right. If you are already married, but you and your mate were heavily involved with each other, deal with that memory of compromise. Verbally, openly, humbly admit your guilt and seek each other's full forgiveness. God will honor such repentance.

Intimacy: It Is Unselfish Affection

The fourth principle, also in I Corinthians 7, is that *intimacy in marriage is an expression of unselfish affection, not selfish desire.*

> *But because of immoralities, let each man have his own wife, and let each woman have her own husband. Let the husband fulfill his duty to his wife, and likewise also the wife to her husband* (vv. 2-3).

What a tremendous difference it made in our marriage when I realized that intimacy in marriage was not simply for my own satisfaction, but for my *wife's* satisfaction. And from her point of view, it wasn't for her satisfaction, it was for *mine.* As Paul describes the "duty," he points out (v. 4) that the wife doesn't have authority over her own body. Clearly, he is referring to a lack of selfishness. She doesn't live with the selfish desire that she is going to be satisfied. She lives with that unselfish desire that her husband is going to be satisfied. Likewise, the husband doesn't have authority over his body, but the wife does. Both parties have a dual role. They are to know pleasure and delight in fulfilling the desire of the other. It works both ways. It's a beautiful way to live.

Two illustrations may clarify this. First, consider the devoted, loving mother who faithfully prepares breakfast, lunch, and dinner for her family, day in and day out. Does she prepare all those meals to satisfy her own hunger? How often does she prepare a meal because the family is hungry? If your family is like ours, *often!* Her drive in carrying out the responsibilities of meal preparation is an unselfish drive that says, "I want to meet their needs." That's what the thought here is.

Or, think of the young man who has a tremendous future in business but decides that God has called him into the ministry. He enrolls in seminary for three or four more years

80   (and takes on an internship) so that someday he might minister. He doesn't do that so that *he* might be satisfied. If he does, it really isn't God's calling at all. He does it so that needs in the lives of other people might be met. It isn't a selfish drive. If it's healthy, it's unselfish. That's how it's to be in marriage — an unselfish giving of oneself.

Intimacy: It Is Uninterrupted

The fifth principle is right here in verse 5: *Intimacy in marriage is not to be interrupted except on very rare occasions.*

> Stop depriving one another, except by agreement for a time that you may devote yourselves to prayer, and come together again lest Satan tempt you because of your lack of self-control (I Corinthians 7:5).

This says that the healthy life and the healthy drive of a healthy husband and wife, however long they've been married, is not to be restrained or squelched, except for three basic guidelines. First of all, by mutual agreement. Second, by a reason serious enough to call for prayer. Third, it should be temporary so that they might come together again.

I'm greatly concerned that this area is lacking in many Christian marriages. I have seen men and women who are tremendous Bible teachers and Bible students, but are feeble in this area of their lives. You may say, "Well, once the Lord takes first place, you really don't need such things as a strong sexual relationship."

God doesn't feel that way. Except on rare instances that drive shouldn't end. A sad witness to that is the great number of men in the ministry whose lives have gone down the moral tube.

The Honeymoon: Why Can't It Begin . . . Again?

Why, though, does the honeymoon end? For some it may be much more complicated than I have described in this chapter. There may be a physical disability or mental disorder. That often calls for professional help. Others of you may be bogged down by ignorance. You are simply uninformed and use incorrect techniques. There are excellent, dependable books available today. Maybe you need to seek the counsel of someone who could wisely help you cultivate and develop this area. Two very excellent cassette tape albums for every married or soon-to-be married person who is searching for a medically accurate presentation of sex in marriage within the framework of the Bible's teaching are recorded by Ed Wheat, M.D., and Gaye Wheat of Springdale, Arkansas, and entitled "Intended for Pleasure" and "Love-Life." Their book, *Intended for Pleasure*, is published by Fleming H. Revell Company of Old Tappan, New Jersey.

Some may be victims of bad or tragic experiences. Perhaps you had a poor relationship with a father or mother. Maybe you were abused or raped. Those hurts must be healed if that is giving you difficulty.

Some may simply be bored, finding intimacy falling into a rut. They have become so set in a routine that the delights and ecstacies of marital love zoom out the window. If you believe in a honeymoon, then I'd suggest you now take a mini-moon. That's spelled M-I-N-I, but it could also be M-A-N-Y. Why not? Is your life so structured that you cannot get away for a weekend periodically without the books or briefcase or children? In our day, we need it. Look, if it was fun to walk on the beach when you were dating, it's fun now. Go do it!

I'm greatly concerned for missionaries who come back on furlough and pack their schedule back-to-back with meetings. They often need a honeymoon! In fact, they need it on the field. And wise are those couples who take time for it.

I find that the honeymoon sometimes ends simply because habits become set in concrete. For no special reason, couples just become disinterested and frigid. God planned intimacy to be warm, exciting, healthy, and growing. Break with the routine. Every once in a while, drop your wife a love note. (You might send a nitroglycerin tablet along with it so she can hold herself together when she gets it!) Pack a note in the suitcase when your husband takes a trip. Tell him what you think.

The other day we had a difficult morning at home. Everything broke loose. We couldn't get the kids to school on time and my wife was crying, the kids were crying, and I felt like crying because I was the cause of most of it. They all left and I was there alone. I sat down and wrote my wife a note:

82   *Darling,*

> *I just want to thank you for all you mean to my life,*
> *for handling the numerous details that free me so I can*
> *do the things that I have to do. You'll never know what*
> *your life means to me. I admire you and I need you.*
> *I love you.*

I thought she would look at it and think, "Hey, that's neat," toss it under the sink, and go right on. Do you know what she did? She taped it on the window in the front of the kitchen sink for all to read! My teenage son came home and spotted that note. As gushy as he could act it out, he read it *out loud.* That's the price you pay for being so romantic.

When did you last send your wife a note? When did you last give her flowers that weren't expected? When's the last time you surprised your loving mate with an expression of affection, wives? Or really caressed him and admitted your passion for him?

Singer Cliff Barrows of the Billy Graham team told me a few years ago about some of the ways he found to maintain delight and happiness in his own home. "I find marriages are held together by twelve words, Chuck," he said. "These are, 'I am wrong,' 'I am sorry,' 'Please forgive me,' and 'I love you.'"

"Hey, that's really good," I told him.

"Well," he replied, "they're not original with me. But I sure find that they work."

That was on Saturday night. On Sunday morning (the next day) I thought, "That would really be good in the sermon." So I shared them. Sunday night I thought, "This will really fit tonight's message." And so I used the list again. Wednesday night Bible study—I thought, "It's amazing how that list fits into this subject." So I rammed it in again. On Saturday we had a wedding at the church. You guessed it. I used the list again in that ceremony.

A lady in our church had been in all four of those services. At the wedding reception she said to me, "Chuck, there are really sixteen words."

"Oh, really?" I said.

"Yes," she replied with a twinkle in her eye. "They are, 'I am wrong,' 'I am sorry,' 'Please forgive me,' 'I love you,' and *This is a recording!*'"

She was right! You can say it like a recording or you can say it like you mean it.

My point in this long chapter is that if you are married and do not experience the delights of intimate love, you're missing the greatest privilege—intimately—that God provides on earth. And if you're missing it regularly, the honeymoon is over.

How about changing things?

How about starting today?

I dare you.

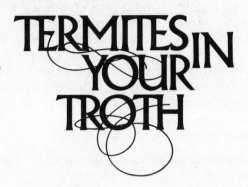

6

TERMITES IN YOUR TROTH

In the 1960s I developed a friendship with a very bright young student at Harvard. If you know anything about the school, you know they prefer only the top layer of the upper crust. He was in that category, intellectually, which always made me wonder why he liked to hang around me. I suppose the old saying is true: opposites attract.

In his intellectualism he had given up what he considered "unnecessary things," like haircuts, baths, deodorant, and toothpaste. But once you got past the smell, he was a terrific guy. Very genuine and sincere. Best of all, a warm heart for the Lord. Strange mixture, this fella. Crummy looking on the outside, but marvelous within. He always looked like he had just crawled out from under a bridge . . . but deep down inside, he was a winner.

Shortly after coming into a relationship with Jesus Christ, he kept other Christians on their toes—asking questions, probing the meaning of expressions and cliches so commonly used by the traditional troops. Some people got turned off. Frankly, I *loved* it! I really have him to thank for helping me forge out some of the finer points of communicating my theology—things I'd not thought through sufficiently. It was a healthy, meaningful relationship both ways.

86   He finally found a young woman with whom he fell in love . . . and before I knew it, they were discussing marriage. Their wedding turned out to be a real mismatch. Not the bride and groom; they fit each other perfectly. Still do. The difficulty was with the minister of the bride's church. He was super-traditional. This couple was supercasual, especially my unkempt friend, the groom. The minister preferred to use a ceremony that was straight from the book, sounding like it came out of either *King Lear* or William Bradford's files.

As the ceremony got underway, the "thees" and "thous" and "heretofores" and "whethersoevers" began to make my friend increasingly more nervous. But the worst part was that he couldn't interrupt and question what was going on. He frowned, fidgeted, looked up, sighed, bit his lip, wound his watch, scratched—the whole bit. I was having the time of my life watching him squirm!

Finally, the vows . . . the part where the preacher spoke and they were to follow the leader.

Dr. Drysdust came out with, "And unto thee I do pledge thee my troth."

That did it. Up till now, he had managed to maintain his composure (which was a minor miracle!), but no longer. The Harvard hotshot said, "I do pledge thee my *what?*"

Remember, this was right in the middle of the ceremony. The pastor flinched (I was now smiling, I must confess) and cleared his throat as he repeated a little louder, "I do pledge thee my TROTH."

"What in the world is my *troth?*"

A conversation followed. It was the only ceremony I've ever heard done in dialogue! But it was also the most understandable part of all as the two men talked back and forth, discussing the meaning of words. I'll never forget that unique evening in New England.

It's because of that wedding I am particularly drawn to the archaic English term, "troth," in my chapter title.

It means "trust." A couple of centuries ago, it was commonly used for the "betrothal trust" between a couple getting married. The idea of a binding, solid commitment throughout time is in the word. As a bride and groom come to the altar, they promise to build their relationship on mutual trust. Or, at least, they *should.* And it is the trust that becomes the bond, humanly speaking, that cements the two together.

My concern is with the little things that gnaw away, weaken, and ultimately destroy a marriage. Like tiny termites in a house.

Since we're thinking about remodeling and restoring marriages in this volume, it's necessary that we address the subject of termites that get into our "troth."

Small Things, Not Big

I'm convinced it's not the big things that weaken a marriage. On the contrary, big problems frequently *strengthen* marriages. The loss of a job, sudden illness, the death of a child, long absences because of military service— these more often than not deepen our love and enhance a relationship.

It's the little things. The slow leaks, not the blowouts. The insidious "pests" we seldom even consider that cut away at the heart of a home until finally, it crumbles as two people walk away.

Needed: An Inspection Report

Turn again to the Song of Solomon, the book we blushed our way through in the previous chapter. In the picturesque language of a lover, the husband is speaking to his wife. It's an intimate scene (most of them are in this book!), one of deep affection, tender and romantic. Listen.

"O my dove, in the clefts of the rock,
In the secret place of the steep pathway,
Let me see your form,
Let me hear your voice;
For your voice is sweet,
And your form is lovely" (2:14).

But then, out of the blue, he declares a warning, a word of caution . . .

88   *"Catch the foxes for us,*
        The little foxes that are ruining the vineyards,
        While our vineyards are in blossom" (2:15).

It's like a cymbal crash in a lullaby. The man, however, is concerned that their "vineyard" (growing, delightful relationship) not be destroyed by "foxes" (those little "termites" that eat away at a relationship). So naturally, like an inspector, he sends out a warning signal. "Catch the foxes!" Or, in light of our analogy, "Kill the pests!" Implied here is the very real fact that pests are always present, always ready to devour the blossoms. The couple that forgets that fact is ripe and ready for an invasion into their vineyard.

You may be surprised to know that more structures are destroyed by termites than by fire each year. Incredible as it may seem, these tiny, silent, industrious insects create greater havoc than the lashing, brutal, headline-making flames of fire.

Four "Termites" That Weaken Marriages

Turn now to the fifth chapter of Ephesians. The last thirteen verses of this grand chapter are perhaps the most familiar words in all the New Testament on marriage. Everything in the chapter builds like a climax to those verses. But I'd like us to back up to verses 15-21, the paragraph just before the finale. It is here we shall find four of the more common termites that weaken the marriage bond.

First, however, read these verses slowly, preferably aloud:

Therefore be careful how you walk, not as unwise men, but as wise, making the most of your time, because the days are evil. So then do not be foolish, but understand what the will of the Lord is. And do not get drunk with wine, for that is dissipation, but be filled with the Spirit, speaking to one another in psalms and hymns and spiritual songs, singing and making melody with your heart to the Lord; always giving thanks for all things in the name of our Lord Jesus Christ to God, even the Father; and be subject to one another in the fear of Christ (Ephesians 5:15-21).*

Confusion

Go back to verse 15 and read it one more time. Paul begins with an imperative, a strong command. "Be careful!" The New International Version says, "Be very careful!" Literally, the Greek terms convey the thought of continuing to take heed how accurately, how exactly you conduct yourself. Here's the idea: "Keep on taking heed how accurately you are conducting your life!" He is pleading for some honest self-analysis. Painful, but needed.

Since we are thinking about marriage, "Keep on taking heed how accurately you fulfill your role as a husband or wife!" In order to accomplish this, you need a ruler, a standard. Without that, you are in a continual state of confusion. Uncertainty abounds. The standard, of course, is your Bible: the reliable, inerrant guide to direct your thought correctly. By turning to this Book you gain a proper perspective, a guideline to follow. The termite of confusion is forced out of your relationship as you gain a clear understanding of your responsibility.

I have observed three major reasons why husbands and wives get confused about their roles in marriage.

First, they are assaulted by the secular propaganda opposed to a monogamous relationship. You listen long enough to garbage like "Marriage is obsolete!" and "Swingers have more fun" and "It's degrading for a woman to be in submission to any man" . . . and before long, you develop what the experts are calling "floating anxieties." That's a four-bit expression for "confusion."

Second, confusion often increases because of the complexity of interpersonal relationships. Let me explain. A husband and a wife enjoy a simple, uncomplicated, one-on-one relationship. This basic interpersonal relationship is relatively easy to maintain—until a child comes on the scene. Suddenly, it jumps to three: husband-wife . . . momma-baby . . . daddy-baby. When *another* child arrives, there are now six interpersonal relationships. If you have four children (as we do), hang on. It jumps to 15. Five children? You have 21 interpersonal relationships bouncing around your pad. You get any more and you'll need to computerize the thing! And how does this add to the confusion? Well, a wife and mother

90   starts asking, "Am I a cook . . . laundry woman . . . chauffeur . . . seamstress? Or mistress . . . partner . . . counselor . . . traveling companion? Or PTA officer . . . financier . . . student . . . Ms. Everything?" Confusion also assaults dad who is beginning his mid-life crisis to boot.

Third, some couples are just plain immature. How many of us have to admit we grew up *after* we got married? I know I did. So did Cynthia. We dated one week before I asked her to marry me. That's right, friends and neighbors, I waited that long so I'd be sure I had the right one. She was 16, I was 18. Really mature, really stable. We married 18 months later. Our children tease their mom by telling others I had to sign her report card. That isn't true. We certainly waited until she got out of high school before we got married. Two weeks. We had the maturity of a couple of nanny goats—and more stubbornness than a whole pen full of 'em.

In 25 years, we've worked through a lot of confusion. And I'll tell you, without a Bible to keep us on course, no way! Take away the Scriptures and I wouldn't predict two years of harmony for any couple . . . for some, not even two months. The confusion termite is a killer. Only God's truth can exterminate it.

Too Busy

         There is another home-wrecker—the too-busy termite. Read Ephesians 5:15-16 again.

Therefore be careful how you walk, not as unwise men, but as wise, making the most of your time, because the days are evil.

Something that is evil is in direct opposition to the good. That describes the day in which we live. Evil. Designed to oppose what is good. Many a couple is caught in the trap of becoming too busy. Not necessarily bad things, just too *many* things.

What a strange species we are! Man is the only animal that runs faster when he loses his way. The result? Increased irritability. Frayed nerves. Impatience. Shorter fuse. Preoccupation. Procrastination when it comes to choosing the right priorities. Yes, such days are "evil." Don't dodge it, face it. Admit it.

Better than that, let's adopt the scriptural injunction and
start "making the most of your time."

In *The Family First* (good title), the author, Kenneth
Gangel, writes convicting words.

> *The man who must travel one hour each way to his*
> *business in the city besides spending eight or nine*
> *hours there, finds himself on the short end of the clock*
> *when it becomes necessary to spend some time with*
> *wife and children. But here again we are dealing with*
> *the matter of priorities. It is not so much a question of*
> *how the husband spends all his time, but rather how*
> *he chooses to spend that time which he can afford to*
> *invest as he chooses.*[1]

That's the kind of thing husbands and wives *must* address.
And it's been my observation that Christian couples are the
worst offenders. For some reason we are beginning to crank
out more workaholics, more high-achieving neurotics, more
nervous, anxiety-prone people than ever before. Many a child
watches with bewilderment as mom and dad ricochet from
room to room in the house, speed to one meeting after
another, cram down Big Macs, often dumping out religious
cliches en route. Who are we kidding? Being too busy is not a
friend, it's an enemy to a home. An evil, selfish, demanding
force that requires things of us, things we have no business
surrendering.

A designer friend of mine, Paul Lewis, who did the cover
design on this book, recently introduced me to an outstand-
ing little book. I sat down and read it in one sitting. It's called
When I Relax I Feel Guilty. Buy it. Read it. Even if you have to
cancel a meeting. Your health deserves it. So does your marriage.

In this fine book by Tim Hansel, a poem by Orin L. Crain
appears that is really worth your time. I share it with you, but I
would add, don't hurry through it. Digest it. Read it—perhaps
twice.

SLOW ME DOWN, LORD[2]

Slow me down, Lord.
    Ease the pounding of my heart by the quieting of
my mind.

Steady my hurried pace with a vision of the eternal reach of time.

Give me, amid the confusion of the day, the calmness of the everlasting hills.

Break the tensions of my nerves and muscles with the soothing music of the singing streams that live in my memory.

Teach me the art of taking minute vacations—of slowing down to look at a flower, to chat with a friend, to pat a dog, to smile at a child, to read a few lines from a good book.

Slow me down, Lord, and inspire me to send my roots deep into the soil of life's enduring values, that I may grow toward my greater destiny.

Remind me each day that the race is not always to the swift; that there is more to life than increasing its speed.

Let me look upward to the towering oak and know that it grew great and strong because it grew slowly and well.

Orin L. Crain

Isn't that penetrating? Believe me, the too-busy termite will ultimately ruin your marriage if you let it remain in your home. It will turn you into a fanatical, determined, stern race horse that is unable (ultimately) to slow down. A prime subject for a coronary. Let me say it directly, pulling no punches. No amount of fanatical zeal or noble calling will ever justify the destruction of a home . . . I don't care how religious the reason or how spiritual the squirrel cage!

Hear the testimony of a former workaholic, get rid of that too-busy termite, *or else.*

Insensitivity

We've considered the confused termite and the too-busy termite. Both are disastrous to a marriage. There's another—the dull termite. Look again at Ephesians 5:17:

So then do not be foolish, but understand what the will of the Lord is.

Centuries before Paul originally wrote these words, the Hebrews had a term for "fool." It was from a verb that meant "dull, insensitive." Like a thick callus impervious to feeling.

The same idea is carried out here in the Ephesian letter. Literally, it's a present imperative, a command, suggesting either "Stop being thick . . .!" or "Don't get into the habit of being thick!" Applying it to a marriage, as we are doing, God is saying, "Quit being so insensitive and inconsiderate of your mate!" Good, wise, needed counsel.

When the dull termite invades a marriage (it usually takes this species a few years), it prompts thinking like, "I'm really not aware of what's happening," or worse, "I really don't care much anymore . . . it's not worth the effort." God says strongly, "Stop thinking like that! Quit it! Break that habit!"

But how?

How can a couple get rid of a dull, insensitive spirit between them? Well, look back at the seventeenth verse. God places a positive immediately after the negative command. The two complement each other.

". . . but understand what the will of the Lord is."

The key to this is "understanding." An old, reliable, New Testament authority states the problem of insensitivity:

". . . the lack of common-sense perception of the reality of things." [3]

God offers a solution—think keenly, using common sense, about what the will of the Lord is for you as a wife, as a husband. Breaking the thick, insensitive barrier in a marriage is tough, but not impossible.

Most every summer the Swindoll family enjoys a week or so at Mount Hermon, a lovely, picturesque, Christian conference grounds nestled in the cool, wooded hillside along the coast near Santa Cruz. Some of our most treasured memories are related to the days we have spent in that delightful setting. A couple of years ago I spoke at a family conference there, and we became acquainted with a family that had come for their first time. The dad was a bright, energetic, up-and-coming young executive with an aggressive firm on the West Coast. His wife was equally intelligent, attractive, and a loving

94   mother of their three children. I spoke that year on the family, drawing various principles out of the Bible and explaining how relevant they were for today. It was a super time. As always, God's Word did the job. Lives were changed.

As the week began to unfold, I started taking special interest in this couple. They reminded me of two hungry baby birds. Each time we gathered for another session, there they were, loving every minute of it, gulping down one biblical insight after another.

Before we left on Saturday they came over to me and embraced me, both of them sobbing audibly. In a brief period of time they spilled out their story. Through tears they admitted they had fallen into this subtle trap of insensitivity. He was preoccupied with his work, climbing the corporate ladder, and determined to get to the top before he turned 50 years of age. She, in turn, compensated by being the super mom, trying to replace the absent father and providing all the things her kids needed. Both were spinning in separate orbits, hardly aware of the other's goals and concerns.

No extramarital affairs. No huge, lengthy arguments, not even a thought of divorce. But separate lives. Like the song, they modeled these words:

"Two different worlds we live in . . . ."

Their growing insensitivity was exposed as they turned to the Scriptures and listened to its counsel on the home. They literally "understood what the will of the Lord is" and they *both* submitted themselves to it. An internal revolution occurred that week in that marriage. For the first time in years they began to listen to and care for and be aware of each other. To use Paul's words, they "stopped being foolish." The dull termite was exterminated in that couple's marriage at Mount Hermon that summer.

Before closing the chapter, there is one more devastating termite that weakens a marriage troth. As soon as I name it, you'll agree.

Stubbornness
            Yes, just plain bull-headedness. The stubborn termite can make a home a hell.

Ephesians 5:18-21 says:

*And do not get drunk with wine, for that is dissipa-
tion, but be filled with the Spirit,*
*speaking to one another in psalms and hymns and
spiritual songs, singing and making melody with your
heart to the Lord;*
*always giving thanks for all things in the name of our
Lord Jesus Christ to God, even the Father;*
and be subject to one another in the fear of Christ.

There's a lot of interesting and important theology here, but
let's try to stick with the subject of marriage since that's what
the passage is leading to in verses 22-33.

Highlight in your mind the last verse, verse 21. It says, ". . .
be subject to one another. . . ." Are you ready for that? *Mutual*
submission is rarely mentioned. The New International Version renders this:

Submit to one another out of reverence for Christ.

That's the secret! The only way the stubborn termite can be
exterminated is through an all-out respect for Christ. Eyes on
Him. A deep, genuine, wholesome reverence for Christ Jesus
as Lord.

Stubborn feelings can be subtle, almost hidden. "I can't
stand it, but I will grit my teeth and bear it. I will live with you,
but don't expect me to cooperate." And on the other hand a
stubborn will can be very obvious and obnoxious. "No way am
I going to give in! This is what I want and it's what I'm gonna
get!" I say a lot about marital fights in the next chapter, but
suffice it to say here, this stubborn resistance creates more
arguments and conflicts than any other single problem in
marriage. The stubborn termite, as it begins to do its damage,
turns holy wedlock into an unholy deadlock. Incompatibility
and anger replace harmony and peace. Misery moves in. In
spades.

Why? Back to verse 21. Because of an unwillingness on the
part of either or both partners to surrender . . . to do precisely
as God has declared.

Operation Extermination

If you're serious about your "troth" and you really want to reaffirm your vows before God, four termites must be exterminated.

1. Confusion

2. Too busy

3. Insensitivity

4. Stubbornness

Here's how. With God's help, you can locate and exterminate. But it will require two-fisted determination.

First, *openly admit the termites have invaded.* Quit denying the truth. As the light of the Word of God has shined brightly, bringing the real facts out of hiding, say so. Deny it no longer. Identify the pest(s) by name. In doing so, admit your culpability, your struggle, your tendency toward that particular problem.

From fourth grade until I entered seminary, my home was in Houston. You know Houston—humidity city! Wall-to-wall bugs. It's unreal. Even though my spotlessly clean mother denied it, our home had roaches. To her, our place was off-limits to those nasty creatures . . . but they apparently didn't get the message. I finally decided to prove to her they were really there. We quietly tiptoed to the kitchen door one night. I snapped on the light and she screamed. Those guys must have been having a rodeo between the range and the refrigerator. Startled, they scattered in all four directions as mother covered her eyes. The light exposed them. From then on she admitted the problem. We had roaches!

Maybe you're a positive-thinking kind of marriage partner. That's okay, just so you're not denying reality. If termites are in your troth, say so! If the light of Scripture has exposed them, the first step toward correction is admission.

Second, *discuss and then determine how you plan to control them.* Being aware of termites then doing nothing about them is ridiculous. Since they are the only insect that never sleeps (even the pest world has workaholics), they stay at the task incessantly. They *must* be controlled. So must the bothersome, irritating, destructive pests in your marriage. Like termites, you may not be able to get rid of them all permanently, but you can certainly exterminate enough to guarantee salvaging your home. Be up front with your partner. Seek some solutions.

Third, *start today.* Not tomorrow. Not when you finish this book . . . or when you make promises to cooperate. No, *now.* Today. Ask your Lord to deal directly with your part of the problem. Please . . . do not put it off.

Remember when you "pledged your troth?" God heard your promise. He smiles on every effort you make to keep that promise . . . to strengthen your trust.

Is He still smiling?

---

[1] Dr. Kenneth Gangel, *The Family First* (Winona Lake, Indiana: BMH Books, 1972), p. 116.

[2] Tim Hansel, *When I Relax I Feel Guilty* (Elgin, Illinois: David C. Cook Publishing Co., 1979), p. 9.

[3] W. E. Vine, *An Expository Dictionary of New Testament Words,* 4 vols. (Old Tappan, New Jersey: Fleming H. Revell Company, 1940), 2:113.

7

HOW TO HAVE A GOOD FIGHT

You will be surprised to know I grew up in a home next door to a boxing ring. That's right, ringside every Saturday night. Preliminary bouts were held during week nights, but the main event was always on Saturday night. Late. Like somewhere between 11:30 and 1:00 in the morning.

The fights were never fair. There was an 11-year-old bantam weight, a welter-weight dad, and (I'll be gracious) a light-heavy-weight mom. What a scene!

When the main event began, the three Swindoll kids would quickly gather in the boys' room, turn off the light, push open the window, and watch it happen. My mother would put on the popcorn and serve it up with cokes or hot chocolate. I'll tell you, it was better than Hawaii Five-O, Kojak, the Rockford Files, and the Dukes of Hazzard all wrapped up into one. It was the best show in East Houston—always unpredictable and exciting. Frankly, I was sorry to see those folks finally move.

Two things stick in my mind when I remember those people next door. First, they owned a radio which served as the ring bell, the gong. When it came flying out onto their screened-in

100 porch, we knew the fight was almost over. Second, they drove a 1941 *Lincoln Zephyr*—a huge, 16-cylinder set of wheels that had no muffler—which always announced their arrival. Soon as we'd hear the screech of the tires and the Sherman-tank roar of their Lincoln, we'd pile up on the bed and stare in childlike wonder.

It began in the driveway around the car with five or ten minutes of chasing. Then one got inside and the lights snapped on. Of course, they had no shades to draw and there were no rules and no bells. It was just hand-to-hand combat from start to finish. It lasted anywhere from ten minutes to one night's record of two hours.

I'll never forget those Saturday nights. After we were sent to bed, I'd lie awake wondering how many families in that vast metropolis were fighting that night.

Fights Are Common

As I grew up, I became friends with a fellow who drove an emergency vehicle for the Mercy Corps, a para-medics organization. At times he took me along and I discovered a lot of other houses were also boxing rings inside.

Even now, I am amazed how often I come across people who fight. Occasionally, the highly educated fight. Even Christians fight. I don't mean people will always fight with their fists, but sometimes that happens, too. A while ago, a born-again Christian man told me that he had great difficulty restraining his anger. It was not uncommon for him to strike his wife and children several times. He was deeply concerned about what prompted that behavior.

If the truth were known, not some, but *most* marriages are marked by periodic skirmishes—occasionally an all-out *war.* Frequently, the marital warfare is in the trenches of belligerence or moodiness. Some battles are "night attacks" or surprise assaults. Others are cold wars of stoic silence. Cruel methods of torture are also employed—public criticism, fearful threats, intimidation, ugly sarcasm, and hateful remarks designed to put down one's mate.

Such tactics are popular . . . but *wrong* because they are unfair and they never lead to domestic peace. It may be impossible to stamp out fighting completely, but in this chapter we want to learn why couples fight, and then what rules can keep it clean, good, and beneficial.

Why Do Couples Fight?

From my years of witnessing fights and the results of those fights in counseling, I've come up with two basic facts about fights. First, most couples don't fight until after they marry. Seldom do you find an engaged couple fighting with each other. Why do things change when people marry? Everything before you say "I do" is voluntary, but after you say "I do," it's compulsory. Right? Beforehand, there is an open end, but afterwards you are boxed in (no pun intended). Furthermore, when people go together, they usually aren't totally honest. They put their best foot forward and act as though they like things they don't.

For example, the girl loves opera and the guy hates it. She sighs, "Oh, I'd love to go see 'Carmen.'" He lies, "Oh, I'd *love* to go, too!" What does he do? He buys two tickets and takes her to "Carmen." He hates every warble of it, but he doesn't say so. After they marry, she says, "Honey, let's go to the opera." He says, "I hate opera!" She doesn't understand why, and if the truth were known, he doesn't understand why he lied before they were married. But he did.

Or, the girl hates fishing, but the guy loves it. Before they're married, he says, "I'll come by and pick you up at 3:30 in the morning and we'll zing down to the lake and fish all day." She gushes (deceitfully), "Wonderful!" So she gets up at 2:30 in the morning, thoughtfully packs a lunch, and piles in the car promptly at 3:30. She's singing and telling him how much she loves him, and they fish all day. Then they get married. Several months later he says, "Honey, let's get up and go fishing." She says, "Not me. I can't stand fishing."

"Why? You used to go."

GONG! The fight starts.

And it even goes deeper. Before the marriage the fellow initiates the love relationship. He's assertive and decisive. She loves it. After marriage he looks upon his bride as someone to take care of him. She is still expecting the role of leadership to

102   flow, but it doesn't. See the problem—why couples often fight not before, but after marriage?

There's another fact we dare not overlook: Most fights are not fair, so no one wins and both lose! In these fights, couples resort to unbiblical, dirty tactics . . . to physical and verbal abuse, slamming one another to the mat with ugly, rejecting statements.

Disagreements are part of marriage. We have to be realistic. Two strong, independent people will not flow together without some turbulence.

Several years ago I visited Pittsburgh and stayed in a hotel that overlooked the confluence of two rivers—the Allegheny and Monongahela. Where those two massive rivers become one larger river, the mighty Ohio River, the current is very strong.

That's how it is in a marriage. When two strong, independent persons flow together at the altar, a lot of power is generated. Suddenly, in some cases, a virtual hell breaks loose and the couple wonders what's wrong. But it is a natural problem that has to be worked through. Fights occur. Few are the couples who can honestly say they've never fought.

Rules On How To Keep It Clean

How can couples flow together in the current and still stay together in harmony? Ephesians 4:25-32 will be the guide to answering this. It offers *seven rules* for having a good fight. These rules will allow you to carry on normal, natural, disagreeable times without breaking with Scripture. If you are the fighting type, I'd urge you to write down the rules and even put them in a prominent place so you can refer to them until they become a part of your life. The scriptural basis:

> *Therefore, laying aside falsehood, speak truth,*
> *each one of you, with his neighbor, for we are members*
> *of one another.*
>   *Be angry, and yet do not sin; do not let the sun*
> *go down on your anger,*
>   *and do not give the devil an opportunity.*
>   *Let him who steals steal no longer; but rather let him*

labor, performing with his own hands what is good,
in order that he may have something to share with him
who has need.

Let no unwholesome word proceed from your mouth,
but only such a word as is good for edification
according to the need of the moment, that it may give
grace to those who hear.

And do not grieve the Holy Spirit of God, by whom you
were sealed for the day of redemption.

Let all bitterness and wrath and anger and clamor
and slander be put away from you, along with
all malice.

And be kind to one another, tender-hearted, forgiving
each other, just as God in Christ also has forgiven you
(Ephesians 4:25-32).

Keep It Honest

Rule one is from verse 25: *Be committed to*
honesty and mutual respect. If you were to read that twenty-
fifth verse as Paul wrote it, it would read: "Therefore, having
laid aside falsehood, talk truth." In Greek there is a particular
verb tense that conveys the idea of something being done in a
point of time. There is a different verb tense to convey the idea
of continued action, going on day after day. The particular
verb here for "laying aside" is the former, rather than the lat-
ter. And when it appears in the sentence with a main verb, it
always precedes the action of the main verb. In other words,
the laying aside is to be done in a point of time . . . and ahead of
the fact that you will now start telling the truth. That's why I
rendered it, "Therefore, *having* laid aside lying, talk truth-
fully."

I'm calling this a commitment because of the thought here
of having already done something. This isn't something that
you do day after day after day. Rather, as a husband to a wife
and a wife to a husband, you commit yourself by saying,
"Honey, no matter what, I want you to know that from this
point and forever in our relationship, it is my deep desire to be
honest with you and to respect you as a person." It is not
something that is repeated in a half-hearted way time and
time again throughout a marriage.

104   Some of you have never made that commitment. At the altar you vowed certain things. But have you ever committed yourself, verbally and honestly in your soul, to being authentic and honest with your partner, viewing your partner with respect? I get the idea of showing respect from the last part of verse 25: "Speak truth, each one of you, with his neighbor, for we are members of one another."

I perform weddings only for people who are born-again— only for Christians. That's because I believe that when you marry another born-again person, you take on not only a wife or husband but also a brother or sister in the faith. You're not just marrying a man or woman; you are marrying another member of the family of God. That adds an essential dimension to your marriage. Just as you would hold in high respect someone sitting in your pew, you would also do the same for your marriage partner. That's why I'm suggesting that there be a commitment of this kind.

It is essential that you commit yourself to an honest relationship, ideally even before you marry, so that you do not fall into the trap of acting, of lying to each other just to win your partner over. I am deeply concerned that couples who date start off right from the beginning with total honesty. They need to say, "Let's not try to kid each other. Let's not play games, I want to be honest with you and I want you to be honest with me. I can take it and I will give it back with tact." Then when fights occur, no one is set up for a surprise punch.

Keep It Under Control

After being committed to honesty and mutual respect, the second rule is: *Make sure your weapons are not deadly.*

Be angry, and yet do not sin (v. 26).

Maybe you have never really understood this verse. Scholars commonly call it a permissive imperative. That means that God is not commanding you to blow your stack. God is permitting you to be angry on certain occasions, but He is warning you not to let it lead to sin, because sin leads to a death-like existence. That's why the weapons of anger can be deadly.

I find a green light in this verse for anger. He says, "I permit you to be angry, but I say to you (with the same stroke of the pen before the ink is dry), don't let that anger lead to sin." All of us know in our consciences when anger has become sin. I don't have to spell that out for you. Bursts of temper are sinful. Anger that slips out of control is sinful. Anger that plans to hurt another member of the family or another individual is sinful anger. Anger that is expressed in profanity is, too. You know the point where your anger becomes sin. That's the point he has in mind.

Proverbs 18:14 tells us why it's important not to have deadly weapons and not to employ deadly words:

> The spirit of a man can endure his sickness,
> but a broken spirit who can bear?

I want you to remember the last part of this contrastive proverb. A man or woman can endure sickness, but they cannot endure a broken spirit. In other places in Proverbs, this is called a crushed spirit. The crushing of the spirit of a child is different from the breaking of the child's self-will. You don't want to do the crushing, but you want to do the breaking. The same is true in a marriage relationship. Verse 19 of the same chapter in Proverbs shows why it's important:

> A brother offended [a wife offended, a husband
> offended] is harder to be won than a strong city,
> and contentions are like the bars of a castle
> [brackets are mine].

Have you ever been wounded or crushed by your mate? I'm sure that we all have at times. Angry words said in the spur of the moment are deadly weapons. When we attack the person rather than the problem, we move into deadly areas. When we make things personal or assault motives rather than dealing with the wrong *situation*, we're treading on thin ice. When we reject rather than reprove, it's harmful.

One man bitterly told me that his father-in-law once announced, "I never did have much use for you after all!" He will never forget that statement until the day of his death. Never. That man used a deadly weapon on his son-in-law. So did the mate who cracked, "No wonder you have a brother in the mental hospital." Or, "I can't stand the way you look." Or,

106 "Those freckles, they're terrible!" Or, "Let's face it, you're ugly, just plain ugly." In a moment of anger, you may actually say that kind of thing, but it's deadly! Your mate may later say, "I forgive you. That's all right. I understand." But deep inside, it's doubtful that will ever be fully forgotten. It's crushing. It breaks that inner spirit that is so much a part of a marriage. Make sure your weapons don't lead to sin. Lay down your deadly arms.

Before coming to the next rule, let me caution you against gross exaggeration. Try to remember to remove the words "always" and "never" from your fights. They have no place because those sweeping universal rebukes are not true. No one "always" or "never" does something. There is an exception somewhere.

Keep It Timed Right

The third rule: *Agree together that the time is right.* This comes after you've committed yourself to honesty and mutual respect and thrown away the deadly weapons so you're now under control. Look at verses 26-27:

> *Do not let the sun go down on your anger,*
> *and do not give the devil an opportunity.*

That's very wise counsel. Paul is not only being specific about not letting anger build up day after day, night after night, but he is implying here the wise use of time. He is suggesting that there is a time in which arguments are to take place. There is the proper time to disagree and there is the proper time *not* to disagree.

Perhaps the most important word in this rule is "together." Be sure that both of you sense that this is the right time to talk. And that's not when husbands come in from work and battle fatigue has set in over his day. Not when wives face a mound of dishes. Or either is fatigued. There are certain times we are not ready to talk in-depth about serious and disagreeable things. Wise are the husbands and wives who know the timing. And if you have that first rule down, you will be honest enough to say, "Honey, this isn't the best time" or "Let's talk a little later when the children are down," or "This isn't the right place to do it. Let's deal with it a little later." And when you say that, keep your appointment. Set the time and don't put it off.

Frequently, couples have battle flags that they wave when they're in need of talking. Mates who are sensitive (last chapter, remember?) learn to read the signals. A husband may become very quiet. A wife may talk rapidly on the phone to her husband and hang up almost before he's through. The husband may show he can't handle more irritation by swearing at the traffic. Your mate may not eat. Or, he bites his fingernails. Get to know those battle flags. Don't let them pass unheeded. Bring the subject up rather calmly. Say, "Could we talk right now, or before long? I'd like us to do it when the time is right." Plan your timing together.

Keep It Positive

Rule four (this is one of my favorites): *Be ready with a positive solution right after taking a swing.* I get this from verse 28. Although Paul is dealing here with the problem of stealing, let's apply the principle to marriage. He makes a statement and then takes a strong swing at it: "Let him who steals, steal no longer." No doubt where he stands on the issue. "I don't want that to go on any longer," he says. "It's wrong before God. There's no way you can justify it. Don't steal." But, he comes right back with a positive, supportive solution:

Rather let him labor, performing with his own hands what is good, in order that he may have something to share with him who has need.

After taking a swing at the problem of stealing, he suggests a healthy, workable alternative: "I'm not going to leave you dangling, telling thieves not to steal. That alone doesn't do any good. I'm going to tell you how you can help it." An elder in a former church used to say, "I won't listen to any criticism in this church if a person doesn't offer, along with the criticism, a suggestion on how we might correct the problem." Not a bad idea! When you come to your mate with justified criticism, be quick with a suggested solution. Criticism hurts. A positive, supportive comment will help take some of the sting out of the wound.

108   This is where I have often been weak in my own marriage. My wife's been with the kids 12 to 14 hours during the day, and I walk in and say, "You're very irritated, aren't you?" That's really a wonderful way to begin an evening with the wife! Or, "Don't get so discouraged. You'll be through with the dishes by eleven o'clock." I soon began to realize that such comments don't do anything but drive the hurt deeper. How much better to say, "Sweetheart, you must be exhausted. Let me work with you in this." Or, "Honey, I've discovered that when I get irritated with our children, this helps."

Coming back with a positive solution helps support the person who is already demoralized in his spirit. Paul is not only telling the thief that it is wrong to steal, he also tells him what to do about it. He says, "Go to work so that you learn the joys of giving, and then you'll not want to steal." Remember: Condemnation without hope crushes.

Keep It Tactful

    Rule five: *Watch your words and guard your tone.* In brief, use tact. This probably will be the most difficult rule to implement because when we have a point to make that we feel very strongly about, we tend to get louder. When we get softer, though, we say more. The louder our voices, the less our mate will hear; the uglier the words, the less we will communicate. Paul says in verse 29:

Let no unwholesome word proceed from your mouth . . . .

"Unwholesome" means "rotten, putrid." It certainly would include profanity and swearing, bitter words. But look at how gracious Paul is. He doesn't just attack. He says, in effect, here's the other side:

. . . but only such a word as is good for edification according to the need of the moment, that it may give grace to those who hear.

You can cultivate such an honest and mutually respected relationship with your mate that both of you can live with a teachable spirit toward one another. But the bond is tactfulness. In his book *Family Communication,* Sven Wahlroos has written one of the finest pieces on tact I've ever read. Here's part of it:

. . . tactfulness is an approach to another human being which involves being sincere and open in communication while at the same time showing respect for the other person's feelings and taking care not to hurt him unnecessarily. Tactfulness involves an implicit trust or faith in the other person and communicates the message: "I trust that you will be able to handle what I'm going to tell you, as long as I respect your feelings and do my best to guard against my own destructive tendencies so that I don't hurt you unnecessarily."[1]

This is profound. With tact, you say, "I trust you and I trust as I share these words I won't hurt you unnecessarily." Unless it's a very unusual situation or your wife or husband is a very unusual person, that will absolutely disarm them if it's said in sincerity.

I have found that our home has its most productive "fights" when that kind of groundwork was laid. We need to say, "Look, honey, I don't personally agree with you right now. I know you don't agree with me, either, but whatever we say from this point on, let's understand, we don't want to hurt the other. We want to come to the right conclusion." And then we get into it. Tact does wonders when it comes to removing a defensive spirit.

Verse 30 says, "Do not grieve the Holy Spirit of God." You understand that when you do sin, whether it's at home in your heart, or in public, you have grieved the Spirit. He says, "Let's not do that."

Keep It Private

The sixth rule for a good fight is: *Don't swing at your mate in public.* That's from verse 31:

Let all bitterness and wrath and anger and clamor and slander be put away from you, along with all malice.

When you swing in public, your malice is showing. There are at least two ways that you can do this in a marriage. First of all, you can do it with open, bold embarrassment. Second, you can do it with subtle, cutting sarcasm. Either one hurts deeply.

110   In a church I formerly served many years ago, a husband was having a great deal of difficulty with his strong-willed wife. As a result, he became increasingly strong-willed as well (this often happens), and their home became a volatile powder keg. One Sunday morning in which I had spoken on living the Christian life at home, he just threw up his arms in despair. He was crushed in his own spirit before God. He was hurt, realizing that he had been wrong to use the same aggressive tactics.

He came to me in the vestibule of the church, which was jammed with probably 50 people. Some were involved in conversations, some were trying to get out, and others were browsing through some literature. He began to share privately the overflow of his hurt, and very quietly admitted to me, "I have caused havoc in our home this week. I confess in my rage I swore at her the other day. I'm embarrassed to admit our home is a wreck. Why, just last Tuesday, I was ready to walk . . . ."

About that time his wife came up. She hadn't heard his confession, his contrite spirit, only the last part where he said, "Our home is a wreck." With a fair amount of volume, she said, "It's because of your *black heart* that our home is a wreck!" The vestibule hushed. As he reddened, she maliciously sliced away at him for everyone to hear. He was devastated. I was embarrassed for him . . . and others blushed and walked away.

You never take your dirty laundry to church to wash it out, do you? Nor do you bring it along to social gatherings, do you? No, you put it where it belongs. You deal with it there. That's where your dirty laundry from a relationship ought to stay. Except in cases of personal counsel with a trusted confidant, don't share the soiled details of your marriage in public. That only succeeds in amassing a group of people who pity you and your terrible plight. Or it embarrasses them. Down in your soul, you know that if your husband or your wife were ever to hear the problems publicly proclaimed, it would only drive the resentment deeper. So don't swing at your mate in public. Put away slander and clamor and all malice.

And let's consider another kind of criticism: *sarcasm*. What a cruel game to play in public! And yet, it is among the favorites. Believe me, others may grin and giggle, but your mate will never forget the slam. I married a dear couple several years ago who felt so strongly against sarcasm they added to their vows a promise before God not to engage in it. Sarcasm is, indeed, an unfair swing at your mate in public. Stop it!

Keep It Cleaned Up

Now the seventh rule: *When it's all over, help clean up the mess.* In verse 32 Paul gives three suggestions for mopping it up:

And be kind to one another, tender-hearted, forgiving each other, just as God in Christ also has forgiven you.

Kindness. Tenderness. Forgiveness. At the heart of the word "kindness" is "grace." Be gracious enough to wipe it off the mental slate. At the heart of "tenderness" is "compassion." Be compassionate enough to weep with the one who's hurt from the fight.

And at the heart of forgiveness is the very person of Jesus Christ who forgave you. The greatest exhibition of forgiveness took place at Calvary. Fully forgive like He did. This clean-up process is all important.

Keep It In Mind

Let's take a quick review of the seven rules.
1. Be committed to honesty and mutual respect.
2. Make sure the weapons are not deadly.
3. Agree that the time is right.
4. Be ready with a positive solution, soon after the swing.
5. Watch your words and guard your tone.
6. Don't swing at your mate in public.
7. When it's over, help clean up the mess. This involves kindness, tenderness, and forgiveness.

There are the rules. Write them down. Memorize them. Talk about them. But most of all . . . keep them.

The Best Way To Stop A Fight

How do you stop most fights? Simple. When you are beaten, surrender. When you are whipped, graciously quit. Remarkable as it seems, some adult married couples can be very poor losers. Very childish. All it takes is three mono-

112 syllabic words: "I am wrong" or "You are right." When you say this, the fight ends. Try that.

The husband comes in and he is all bent out of shape and starts to blast away.

You say, "Honey, you are right."

"What did you say?"

"You are right." Genuinely admit it and watch him melt.

Our family had a miniature schnauzer. One time this dog nearly led to a fight in our marriage. She was a female and so it came time to lock her up in the garage.

My wife said, "I really think Heidi needs to stay in the garage. I don't care if it's for a week or two weeks. We'll just have to clean up after her. That's just part of it."

I said, "I don't think that is the best plan. I think that dog needs to be outside a little. She's going to get cabin fever inside that garage. She needs to be able to enjoy being outside."

My wife said, "We're going to have trouble."

I said, "It will work out great. We'll keep our eye on her."

One Monday I was working out in the garage and she was enjoying being outside. I took a quick trip to the hardware store to get some things and when I came back I spotted a big black dog, crawling over our backyard wall with that satisfied look on his face.

I thought, "Oh, no!" I decided, "I'm not going to tell anybody anything." So I didn't. I just let it go. I said to myself, "Nothing happened. Everything is great. It's just my imagination."

And guess what. Yep. Heidi was pregnant. I had to say to my wife, "You were right. I was wrong."

And you know what? Now, it's funny. It's no longer a fight, because one of us is willing to say, "You were right." It's that simple.

You're not going to believe this, but I was in junior high school before I realized the North actually won the Civil War. In fact, some places in the South are still fighting the crazy thing. Why? It's hard for losers to give in.

As one of my close friends in Texas declares: "Those Yankees didn't win . . . we just ran out of ammunition, food, and men!"

How much better to say, "Okay, you win."

Fight all you want to, as long as you keep the rules. They will help you go on to better things. As soon as you are beaten, surrender! Only then are you able to go on.

The alternative requires turning your home into another boxing ring. And take it from me, that's no way to live. Fights belong in big, smoke-filled auditoriums, not in a house that claims to model the message of God's peace.

If you must fight, fight fair and clean. The least you can do is make it a *good* fight!

8

'TIL DEBT DO US PART

Like giant containers of volatile gas, money *must* be handled by married couples with extreme care. Unfortunately, more often than not, our financial posture can be described in six words:

Bad mistakes

Big bills

Bank loans.

Two young adults I married over five years ago (we'll call them Ron and Becky) seemed to be an intelligent, diligent couple with above average common sense. In our premarital counseling sessions, we discussed their finances. In my standard approach, I not only warned them against over-extending themselves, but I also shared some of the principles my wife and I employ. Ron seemed to have a good handle on the subject and Becky made several comments that assured me her head was screwed on straight. I was comfortable with the thought that the two of them would be wise and careful, employing a lot of sense with their dollars.

Becky told me recently she needed to talk with me about the growing distance between Ron and her. As she unveiled the

116   story, I soon realized that poor money management was one of the major contributors to their disharmony.

They had wanted a home—a new one. They found their "dream" and realized quickly it was going to require a chunk of money just to get it in their name . . . plus huge monthly payments of almost $900. At 13.5 percent interest. Over and above this they planned to furnish most of the rooms, drape the windows, build a few extras in the garage, and landscape both front and back yards. Oh, yeah, they also wanted to put up a fence. They decided to finance most of those things.

Becky went to work. Ron added a second job to his busy schedule . . . and, in addition, he worked most weekends with yet another type of employment. Obviously, he was seldom home. Strangely, the very thing they wanted so badly became an empty showcase, a place to sleep, bathe, dress, and choke down a hurried breakfast. By the way, Ron left at 6:00 a.m. and dragged in around 11:30 p.m. Seven days a week. Twelve months a year. Becky was working 40 hours a week, sometimes more.

Becky got pregnant. Two weeks before delivery she quit her job. The baby increased their financial pressure, especially since it led to her unemployment. Within another eighteen months, another pregnancy.

Picture it. A weary, young mother with two in diapers. An incredibly busy husband and father, at home only between midnight and six o'clock in the morning. And that new home neither of them has ever really enjoyed. The payments are constant. And one of the babies is currently ill. Anybody wonder why Becky and Ron are beginning to feel a distance between themselves?

Bad mistakes

Big bills

Bank loans.

Common Problem: Mismanagement

The story can be repeated in America thousands of times. The figures and geography may differ, but not the pressure. By the way, a young executive recently told me that his house payment was *$1800 a month.* That's well over

$20,000 a year just for their house. They, too, are feeling the pinch.

Small wonder one expert states that, "Nine out of every ten people with an income are financial failures." He doesn't mean they declare bankruptcy or they have bad credit or they don't make enough money. He means they fail to manage their money wisely. It's not really a question of dishonesty or lack of diligence, but rather *mismanagement.*

Candidly, I have a personal motivation for emphasizing financial wisdom in this book on marriage. A few months after we got married, Cynthia and I were living on beans and cornbread, with cornbread and syrup for dessert, partly because we had made a bad mistake in an investment. It all happened in 1955. I remember it well.

A man who advertised himself as a stockbroker had come to our area. Many of us who didn't know better were attracted to his smart appearance and his slick portfolio filled with official-looking charts, credentials, and letters of recommendation.

He calmly (and convincingly) explained a plan that would ultimately make us financially independent—for an initial investment of only $600. The dividends would just pour in! Well, $600 to us then would be like $15,000 today . . . but we got it! And he left town.

For good.

That was it. That crook ripped us off and split the scene. The whole deal was a fraud. One of the reasons I joined the Marine Corps shortly after that was to learn how to kill—just in case I met up with that phony some day.

But one thing good came out of our $600 mistake. We learned the value of being good stewards of our money. We discovered (the hard way) that unless we deal wisely with the finances God entrusts to our care, we will pay a terrible price. Mismanagement, quite frankly, is a sin.

Scriptural Reproof

The Bible is a remarkable book. I continually am amazed at its breadth. When it comes to finances, it

118 offers workable principles for living that include earning, buying, borrowing, saving, giving, and investing our money. Not even God Himself breaks these guidelines—except in a very few miraculous exceptions. Couples who wish to get their finances squared away must—I repeat, *must*—seek the counsel of Scripture. There are also some very reliable books[1] you would be wise to read and heed. But most of all, God's Word is the primary and most dependable resource to turn to.

Just listen to a few related passages on the subject of money.

Several in Proverbs are:

A false balance is an abomination to the Lord,
But a just weight is His delight (11:1).

In all labor there is profit,
But mere talk leads only to poverty (14:23).

He who profits illicitly troubles his own house,
But he who hates bribes will live (15:27).

The rich rules over the poor,
And the borrower becomes the lender's slave (22:7).

Do not weary yourself to gain wealth,
Cease from your consideration of it.
When you set your eyes on it, it is gone.
For wealth certainly makes itself wings,
Like an eagle that flies toward the heavens (23:4-5).

Know well the condition of your flocks,
And pay attention to your herds;
For riches are not forever,
Nor does a crown endure to all generations (27:23-24).

Solomon also wrote:

He who loves money will not be satisfied with money,
nor he who loves abundance with its income. This too is
vanity (Ecclesiastes 5:10).

Jesus said these familiar words:

Then the Pharisees went and counseled together how
they might trap Him in what He said.
And they sent their disciples to Him, along with the

Herodians, saying, "Teacher, we know that You are
truthful and teach the way of God in truth, and defer to
no one; for You are not partial to any."
"Tell us therefore, what do You think? Is it lawful to
give a poll-tax to Caesar, or not?"
But Jesus perceived their malice, and said, "Why are
you testing Me, you hypocrites?
"Show Me the coin used for the poll-tax." And they
brought Him a denarius.
And He said to them, "Whose likeness and inscription
is this?"
They said to Him, "Caesar's." Then He said to them,
"Then render to Caesar the things that are Caesar's;
and to God the things that are God's."
And hearing this, they marveled, and leaving Him,
they went away (Matthew 22:15-22).

And Paul added:

For because of this you also pay taxes, for rulers are
servants of God, devoting themselves to this very thing.
Render to all what is due them: tax to whom tax is
due; custom to whom custom; fear to whom fear; honor
to whom honor.
Owe nothing to anyone except to love one another;
for he who loves his neighbor has fulfilled the law
(Romans 13:6-8).

and,

Now this I say, he who sows sparingly shall also reap
sparingly; and he who sows bountifully shall also reap
bountifully.
Let each one do just as he has purposed in his heart;
not grudgingly or under compulsion; for God loves
a cheerful giver.
And God is able to make all grace abound to you,
that always having all sufficiency in everything,
you may have an abundance for every good deed
(2 Corinthians 9:6-8).

And finally,

And if we have food and covering,
with these we shall be content.

120

> *But those who want to get rich fall into temptation and a snare and many foolish and harmful desires which plunge men into ruin and destruction.*
>
> *For the love of money is a root of all sorts of evil, and some by longing for it have wandered away from the faith, and pierced themselves with many a pang.*
>
> *Instruct those who are rich in this present world not to be conceited or to fix their hope on the uncertainty of riches, but on God, who richly supplies us with all things to enjoy.*
>
> *Instruct them to do good, to be rich in good works, to be generous and ready to share,*
>
> *storing up for themselves the treasure of a good foundation for the future, so that they may take hold of that which is life indeed* (I Timothy 6:8-10, 17-19).

Seven Wrong Attitudes

As I think deeply about those great statements from God's Book and then call to mind the attitudes I have witnessed among married couples I have talked to, what a contrast! If I were to summarize them into a list, I believe I could name seven attitudes commonly found in Christian homes:

1. That part is God's money; this part is mine.
2. God really isn't concerned with "secular" things.
3. Let's not get fanatical. Leave God at church.
4. Financial prosperity is suspect—profit-making is unspiritual.
5. Having little is more spiritual than having much.
6. Don't sweat it, some day our ship will come in.
7. God isn't fair! The rich get richer and the poor get poorer.

All seven are wrong.

Not one of these attitudes squares with Scripture. Any marriage that operates from one or more of these concepts is headed either for trouble or, at best, for less than God has designed for us to enjoy.

A Relevant Parable For Today

Several years ago God opened my eyes to a passage of Scripture in Luke 19 that has really helped me to view the management of my finances as *He* views it. This passage is a parable Jesus spoke regarding a prophetic issue I won't get into—I'll just deal with its insights related to money. As we'll see, it offers seven facts that correct the wrong attitudes we just considered.

I have in mind Luke 19:11-26. To set the stage, let's read verses 11-12 first. I'll use the New International Version for the sake of clarity:

> *While they were listening to this, he went on to tell them a parable, because he was near Jerusalem and the people thought that the kingdom of God was going to appear at once. He said:*
> *"A man of noble birth went to a distant country to have himself appointed king and then to return. So he called ten of his servants and gave them ten minas. 'Put this money to work,' he said, 'until I come back,'"*

Obviously, His own departure and return were in Jesus' mind. That prophetic thought is woven throughout the parable. He is the "man of noble birth" and the servants we are going to read about are His followers, people like you and me. So much for the prophetic part—now let's zero in on the practical.

Managing God's Money

> *"So he called ten of his servants and gave them ten minas. 'Put this money to work,' he said, 'until I come back'"* (v. 13).

Here's the first fact that counteracts the wrong attitude I mentioned earlier—

Everything we have has come from God.

This verse states He gave them all the money they were to have. By the way, a "mina" was about three months' wages. Being servants, they possessed nothing apart from the nobleman's provision. Nothing. Servants in those days were totally dependent upon their masters for everything.

You and I are like that. It is incorrect to think that our part is the whole thing minus God's part. No way. Everything we

122 possess, from the coins in our pockets to the savings in the bank, belong to Him. In actuality, the Christian doesn't "own" anything. He or she simply manages God's money. What we handle is entrusted to us from God's hand. This is basic. You will never get a handle on a proper (biblical) perspective of your finances, my friend, until you grasp this foundational fact.

Destroying Secular-Sacred Distinctions

Now, back to the story. After giving each servant the same amount of money, He told them, "Put this money to work . . . until I come back." The Greek verb conveys the idea of "doing business." It is *pragmateuomai*, from which we get "pragmatic." It's a practical, pragmatic command. "Carry on with business until I get back."

Second fact: *In God's eyes, there is no "secular" and "sacred" distinction.*

It is totally inaccurate for you and your marriage partner to think that your business life (stuff that occurs outside church affairs) is of little or no interest to God. When our Lord says "do business," He doesn't mention categories. All of our dealings are of utmost interest to our Lord.

It's wise mentally to "ordain" everything to Him and His service. If you're a teacher, you're an "ordained teacher." A homemaker? Then you're an "ordained homemaker." If you are thinking about investing in something, view that as an "ordained investment."

Why? Because it is His money. And you are carrying on business for Him. The Lord is extremely interested in how we do business. How we budget, how we plan, spend, and save. We are to be as adept in keeping our books as we are in preaching and teaching His Word. He is equally as interested in the way we handle the payroll in our private business as He is in the way we handle His Word. There's no secular-sacred distinction. Remember that!

Doing Business God's Way

Let's read on:

"But his subjects hated him and sent a delegation after him to say, 'We don't want this man to be our king'" (v. 14).

Fact three is clear:

Doing business God's way is contrary to man's way.

The citizens mentioned here are not to be confused with His servants. They represent the inbred worldliness in all of us. You know, that part of us that craves selfish satisfaction. Doing our own thing our own way.

In this parable these subjects said they didn't want His lordship. "We hate Him—we resent His trying to control this part of our lives. This is *our* business!"

Sound familiar? Perhaps you feel like that. You may read this book from cover to cover and intellectually agree with the principles it sets forth. But deep down in your soul—down where those gutsy decisions are made—you really don't have any plans to change your comfortable, present habit patterns. You don't want Him to be your King and to reign over you. You just want to get what you want out of life. Let me level with you. That is rebellion and resistance. It's carnality in the raw. And I can assure you your marriage will not improve until you submit to him.

When he returns, the nobleman asks his slaves, "How did things go?" Look at verse 15:

"He was made king, however, and returned home. Then he sent for the servants to whom he had given the money, in order to find out what they had gained with it" (v. 15).

What was the nobleman concerned about? Business. He wasn't concerned about differences or divisions in segments of the land. He wanted to know, "How was business? Were you wise in managing the money?" Then look at the response in verse 16:

"The first one came and said, 'Sir, your mina has earned ten more' " (v. 16).

Underline the word "your." Not "my" mina, Lord, but *yours*. "Lord, Your salary provided this. Your financial provision for promotion made this possible for us as a family. Lord, your money has prospered me in this way and as I stand before You, here's my accounting of it."

124   " 'Well done, my good servant!' his master replied.
'Because you have been trustworthy in a very small
matter, take charge of ten cities' " (v. 17).

What a tremendous reward!

Pleasing God With Money Management

"The second came and said, 'Sir, your mina has
earned five more' " (v. 18).

A mina was worth about $20. By wise investment he turned
his $20 into $100. Another reward: authority over five cities.

The master was pleased with the servant's initiative, which
introduces the fourth fact:

Wise management of money pleases the Lord.

Some "superspiritual saints" spread rumors that financial
success is suspect. They say profit-making is unspiritual. I
cannot find a biblical basis for that. Certainly, how we use it is
important, but making it is not, in and of itself, unspiritual.
This nobleman came back and asked, "What did you do?"

"I earned more than you gave me."

"Wonderful. Ten cities are for you."

It seems obvious to me he was pleased with the profit.

We have to be careful what that profit means to us. We're not
to amass fortunes for ourselves, to hang on, look at, love, and
selfishly enjoy. Earlier in this chapter, we read warnings from
both Solomon and Paul.

Rather, should fortune come, we are to be willing to turn
around and give it away. That's the difference. The selfish
man gets it so that he might keep it. The born-again individual gets it so that he might release it to those in need . . . and
wisely invest it in so many other areas.

I've said all my life, and I believe it more now than ever, that
the happiest people on planet earth are not the keepers. They
are the givers. The man who received a mina and through
wise management earned tenfold pleased his lord. And the
nobleman turned right around and rewarded him. Wouldn't
God do the same with us?

Displeasing God Without Money Management

There is one more slave to report in:

"Then another servant came and said, 'Sir, here is
your mina; I have kept it laid away in a piece of cloth.
I was afraid of you, because you are a hard man. You
take out what you did not put in and reap what you did
not sow.'

"His master replied, 'I will judge you by your own
words, you wicked servant!' " (vv. 20-22).

Wait a minute, nobleman. He didn't lose it, he's still got it. The one that had $20 wound up with the same $20 later. But the Lord says, "That's not wise," meaning, "I'm not pleased that you just sat on it. I expect you to invest it so it increases in value."

The man had his excuse ready: "I was afraid of you, lord." but his excuse didn't hold water.

Through this slave we find the fifth fact:

Poor management displeases the Lord.

This dispels the common attitude that having little is more spiritual than having much. Where is that idea found in the Bible? Or the thought that God loves the poor more than He loves the rich? I don't believe that. Having riches carries with it a temptation and responsibility the poor never wrestle with. But nowhere in Scripture do I find that being financially prosperous is unspiritual.

Disciplining Your Investment Efforts

Notice what the nobleman asks next:

" 'Why then didn't you put my money on deposit,
so that when I came back, I could have collected it with
interest?' " (v. 23).

That's a good question, isn't it? The Lord offers a low-risk alternative to doing nothing: putting it in a bank so that the principal earns interest. That brings us to the sixth fact:

Management and disciplined planning go hand-in-hand.

An investment plan takes discipline to maintain. And discipline without a plan is frustration. They go together.

126   That means ignorance is *not* bliss. We can't sigh, "Some day our ship will come in." We can't close our eyes and put it on the credit card. READ THAT SENTENCE AGAIN.

By the way, I'm not against credit. I understand that our economy is such that we would be in trouble without credit. I don't understand all that I should about economics, but I do understand that the interest factor works in our favor when properly held in check. My great concern is the unwise over-spending so many couples carry on that breaks their relationship and reveals poor discipline. Here the Lord says, "Look, the least you could have done is deposit it in the bank so it could draw interest."

Losing and Learning

Now, look closely at the following two verses:

"Then he said to those standing by, 'Take his mina away from him and give it to the one who has ten minas."
" 'Sir,' they said, 'he already has ten!' " (vv. 24-25).

Does that seem fair? He's giving it to the fellow who already has a lot! But the Lord says:

" 'I tell you that to everyone who has, more will be given, but as for the one who has nothing, even what he has will be taken away' " (v. 26).

I believe this shows that God blesses wise management, but poor management sees dwindling returns. This seventh fact is the most difficult:

Losses and gains provide eternal lessons.

Our problem is that we don't learn our lessons when we lose or gain. We live in some kind of spiritual dream world, thinking that somehow, in some marvelous way, it's all going to float down in our favor. But God has devised laws and principles for living which include spending, buying, borrowing, saving, and investing.

Learning, Earning, Yearning

The book of Proverbs is filled with maxims about the wisdom of the diligent man. Many of those proverbs imply wisdom in money management. The disciplined, diligent man will be blessed. The one who lacks diligence will become the slave of the lender. (Look again at Proverbs 22:7.) This applies to us when we're earning the least money of our lives and when we've hit our peak earning period. In fact, our earning power could be graphed as a semicircle, low when we're 20 to 30 years of age, rising to a peak in the middle years, and slacking off in retirement.

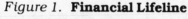

Figure 1. **Financial Lifeline**

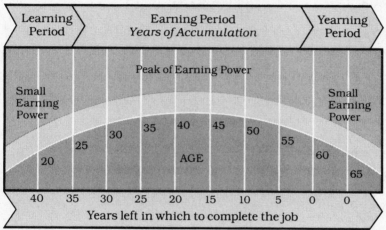

Let's call that first period of earning power the "learning period." One of the great breakdowns in our society is the failure of parents to teach their children how to manage their money. Maybe parents will pass on a couple of important lessons they've learned (believe me, my kids have heard the story of my "investment" enough times!), but they don't ground their children well in basic financial planning.

Our earning power also shrinks when we're 60 or older. Call this the "yearning period."

128   In the middle of life, ages 30 to 60, we reach the peak. This is our "earning period." Think, though, of your age in terms of how many years you have left to plan wisely for your family, parents. When you are 20, you have 40 years left. When you're 30, just as you're moving into the higher-income time, you have only 30 years left. When you hit 40, you have 20 years left. By the time you've reached 50, there are 10 years (give or take a few) left to plan those investments.

Only the Lord knows how set in concrete we really are by the age of 45 or 50 to rethink our finances. You don't have an eternity ahead of you to plan these things. Everything may seem terribly spiritual until suddenly a man leaves a widow and a bunch of children, with no financial assistance. When she is jolted back to reality, she knows they should have planned. As a pastor who ministers to the dying and the grieving, I see this often.

The Bible and Financial Planning

I find four scriptural principles for financial planning. The first is tucked away between the lines of Matthew 22:15-22:

> Then the Pharisees went and counseled together how they might trap Him in what He said.
> And they sent their disciples to Him, along with the Herodians, saying, "Teacher, we know that You are truthful and teach the way of God in truth, and defer to no one; for You are not partial to any.
> "Tell us therefore, what do You think? Is it lawful to give a poll-tax to Caesar, or not?"
> But Jesus perceived their malice, and said, "Why are you testing Me, you hypocrites?
> "Show Me the coin used for the poll-tax." And they brought Him a denarius (vv. 15-19).

That little denarius they held up in front of His face was smaller than an American quarter, though worth about a day's wages. Jesus looked at the impression on the coin and said, "Whose likeness and inscription is this?" What's stamped on this coin?

> They said to Him, "Caesar's." Then He said to them, "Then render to Caesar the things that are Caesar's; and to God the things that are God's" (v. 21).

Pay your taxes if you are deriving benefit from the government, but give God the things that are God's. Simple answer. Let's look at the implications.

On Taxes and Tithes

It's interesting that this passage is always used to describe the biblical necessity of paying one's taxes. But we seldom have someone emphasize the ending of the sentence about rendering to God the things that are God's. We live and die by the joke that nothing is really certain in life except taxes and death. But there *is* something else. God's part. We are to "render," he says, which means "pay back." The Greek verb means "to return." Remember that primary axiom? Everything we have is *His*. Just as we are to pay taxes and just as we must die, we must also give God His part.

The first principle here is: *Christ and Caesar are essential, not optional.* You can't live very long in this world without paying taxes. If you try to ignore them, they catch up with you. The same is true of the Lord's part. If you are involved in a church and deriving a major benefit from it for your family or your own life, then the majority of your contribution should go there.

Often people give as though they were serving out pumpkin pie. They cut up their giving into a number of different pieces and a small part winds up in the church. But the rest is sent elsewhere. Some of that certainly is appropriate. That's the only way many needy ministries could continue. My concern is with the optional feeling many people have toward giving to the local church.

We never think of taxes as optional; Caesar gets his part. But Christ is also to get His part and it is to be planned for. Carefully. Thoroughly. Consistently. Yet how often, when the plate's being passed, do we dig hastily into our pockets and grab something to drop in? At the same time I know men who spend hours and days planning ways to reduce their taxes.

God's part also needs time to be planned out. After all, He is to take first place in our life (Colossians 1:18). The benefits and blessings that are derived are incredible and can never be paid back. Christian couple—give God His part!

130 Back-to-Back Borrowing

The second principle comes from Romans 13:6-8, a passage I've wrestled with for a long time:

> *For because of this you also pay taxes, for rulers are servants of God, devoting themselves to this very thing.*
> *Render to all what is due them: tax to whom tax is due; custom to whom custom; fear to whom fear; honor to whom honor.*
> *Owe nothing to anyone except to love one another; for he who loves his neighbor has fulfilled the law.*

I have debts, as you have debts, yet verse 8 said that I am to owe nothing to anyone except to love him. I've been tempted at times just to send our creditors some notes saying, "I love you very much." With no remittance enclosed. Somehow, I don't think they would accept my love note as a substitute.

"Owe nothing to anyone except to love one another." What does that mean? Is it wrong for a couple to invest and borrow for a home or some large expenditure? Or take out small loans? When Dallas Theological Seminary was making expansion plans, I talked with its president, Dr. John F. Walvoord, about this very point. His answer was a wise one.

"If you look closely," this president-scholar said, "you will notice that the imperative is in the present tense. The thought is 'don't keep on owing.'"

In other words, don't stack up your loans back-to-back so that you never have a break. Pay them off. Don't prolong the debt. Hence the second principle:

Buying and borrowing demand short accounts, not long ones.

Nothing needs to be watched more closely than credit buying. In my premarital counseling with couples I mentioned earlier, one of our sessions deals with the matter of not getting head over heels in debt. Some couples stack up the bills before the knot is even tied with elaborate and expensive plans. These quickly plunge them into the financial pits and soon they have thousands of dollars of "wants" overwhelming them. The only solution is to insist on short accounts.

"Saving Up" Instead Of "Dreaming On"

The third principle is that *savings and security require planning, not dreaming.* Proverbs 14:23 says:

> *In all labor there is profit,*
> *but mere talk leads only to poverty.*

If you want a savings account to build up security for investment, don't just talk and dream about it. A plan will never come to fruition unless it is put into operation.

My wife and I are working toward aligning our family budget according to the guidelines in figure 2. Your total earnings are represented on the top. Out of the total earnings, the Lord is first, then comes taxes to the government. That which remains is what I call the "working money." From there, allow 10 percent for savings and investments, 70 percent for living expenses, and 20 percent for debts and a buffer fund to handle those unexpected items.

Figure 2. **A Suggested Financial Formula***

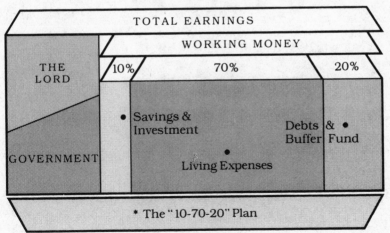

132   I am indebted to Bowman's book *How to Succeed With Your Money* and for his excellent suggestions for working within this framework. You might also seek financial advice from someone you respect, such as your banker. Go to men of integrity whose expertise is money and investment. You'll be wiser to seek their counsel, because savings and securities need intelligent planning, not hopeful dreaming.

How Much Is Too Much?

The fourth and final principle of financial planning is this:

Things and treasures are temporal, not eternal.

Paul's first letter to Timothy tells why:

And if we have food and covering, with these we shall be content (6:8).

It will help emphasize the truth if you will change the word "shall" to "should." That would be more realistic. Having food and covering, we *should* be content. Alas, we often are not. We start thinking our treasures will last forever and we want to pile them up.

But those who want to get rich fall into temptation and a snare and many foolish and harmful desires which plunge men into ruin and destruction. For the love of money is a root of all sorts of evil (I Timothy 6:9-10).

Money is not evil, but the love of it—the idolatry of the coin—is.

Born-again, wealthy people whose hearts are right, however, are to be generous and ready to share—

. . . storing up for themselves the treasure of a good foundation for the future, so that they may take hold of that which is life indeed (I Timothy 6:19).

"Life indeed," if I could paraphrase, is "really living." The man, woman, or couple occupied only with money, money, money have missed what it really means to live.

Well, that's it. Big subject, isn't it? Lots to think about. But if we don't, our marriages suffer. In fact, many of them will fail.

I wish someone would have pulled me aside twenty-five 133
years ago and helped me understand these things. Really!
Maybe that's why I've written such a long chapter . . . to keep
you from struggling as much as I have with finances.

Now that I've got a biblical handle on the subject, I am much
more at ease, much less fearful. Alas, for many couples, however, long before death separates them, debts will.

It need not be.

---

[1] I have found a great deal of help from four particular books. All four are based on
scriptural principles and therefore are reliable resources to consider: *How to Succeed
with Your Money*, George M. Bowman, Moody Press; *You Can Be Financially Free*,
George Fooshee, Jr., Fleming H. Revell Company; *Handbook for Financial Faith-
fulness*, Floyd Sharp and Al Macdonald, Zondervan Publishing House; *Your Money:
Frustration or Freedom?* Howard L. Dayton, Jr., Tyndale House Publishers, Inc.

[2] George M. Bowman, *How to Succeed with Your Money* (Chicago: Moody Press,
1960), p. 71.

[3] George M. Bowman, p. 129.

9

DIVORCE: WHEN IT ALL COMES TUMBLING DOWN

Up 'til now, this has been an enjoyable book to write.

We've consulted the Architect of the home and discovered His original blueprint for getting it all together. We've repaired the foundation by returning to that great passage in Genesis 2 and learning about severance, permanence, unity, and intimacy. We have studied about those necessary bricks that build a marriage, how to keep our honeymoon from ending, ways to handle our conflicts, and even some tips on wise money management.

Written across every page has been the word HOPE. We have openly admitted our imperfections and we have willingly declared our need for divine assistance. Every major point and principle have been affirmed by Scripture . . . so we have not built a case on human opinion. Time and again we have returned to the "original match" to analyze, compare, observe, and learn. We have been reassured that there is no marital problem so great that God cannot solve it. Rebuilding and rekindling have been the recurring theme. No marriage—no matter how weak or scarred—need end.

136   I again agree with my friend in San Francisco. Two processes ought never be entered into prematurely: embalming and divorce. Time and again I have suggested ways in which a marriage can be salvaged. Because I firmly believe there is *nothing* impossible with God. Because I have seen Him turn numerous husbands and wives around—180 degrees. Because it was never His original design that homes be destroyed. And because His Word is filled with promises that hold out hope to those who have blown it. But . . . .

Divorce still occurs. Now, more than ever. Often against the desire of one of the partners. Often in spite of assistance, effort, and much prayer by friends. Often between two Christians—yes, often. And always where biblical principles were unknown, ignored, or openly violated. Nevertheless, divorce happens. It's a fact we may hate (I confess, I really do!), but one we cannot deny.

And so, instead of dodging divorce and acting like it's not there, I've decided to write a chapter that faces it squarely. Even though I would much prefer not to, I haven't that option.

I will be brief (there are entire *books* written on the subject), biblical, and compassionate. But in spite of these efforts, I'm sure some of you will be offended and others will misunderstand. Such is inevitable, unfortunately.

A Controversial Subject

I'm convinced that there is no way any group of Christians picked at random would ever come to unanimity on this subject. I'll go further. I don't believe a bus load of American evangelical theologians would be in unanimous agreement on divorce and remarriage even if they toured the United States an entire summer! It's a controversial issue, for sure. Therefore, no matter what I may conclude, I am confident some very reliable, competent, and equally sincere people will disagree. So save your cards and letters!

I am also confident of this. It's time some of us in the evangelical camp came up front and addressed the issue boldly. Many a divorced person is grinding out his or her life under an enormous load of unnecessary guilt. While I certainly would not desire to soften the penetrating blows of the Spirit of God (if, in fact, it *is* the Spirit producing conviction), I do hope that my words provide the breathing room God has allowed in certain instances. Of greatest concern to me is that someone might read these pages and *misinterpret* what I am saying. Disagreement is one thing; misinterpretation is another. And the emotions surrounding something as stressful as divorce have a way of playing tricks on one's mind, increasing the possibility of misinterpreting what one reads.

Let's make a deal. I promise to be as accurate, clear, and concise as I can possibly be with what I write if you will be equally as careful with what you read. Work hard at not reading into this something I am not saying . . . or take to an extreme something I am trying to keep in proper balance. In issues as controversial as this one, the vehicle of communication must be finely tuned. Let's both do our part, okay?

Not In God's Original Blueprint

It should surprise no one that divorce was never in the original blueprint for the home. Not only is that implied in the Genesis account, it is clearly stated by Jesus:

> *"Because of your hardness of heart, Moses permitted you to divorce your wives; but* ***from the beginning it has not been this way*** *[emphasis mine] (Matthew 19:8).*

The original match was simple and clear: one man (Adam) with one woman (Eve) joined together in a permanent union (marriage) throughout life. How perfect! Yes, and how innocent! Remember, sin was not yet present. Nor a carnal nature within human life. In the beginning days of the home, (think of it !), there was absolute perfection.

Man was totally innocent. Uncontaminated. As we read in Genesis 5:1-2:

> . . . *In the day when God created man,*
> *He made him in the likeness of God.*
> *He created them male and female, and He blessed*
> *them and named them Man in the day when they*
> *were created.*

Clear enough, isn't it? Sinlessness. God's likeness infused into two human beings. The very image of God was stamped upon His creation.

STRIKE THE ORIGINAL MATCH

Sin's Shattering Effect On Marriage

But wait. Read on. In the same chapter, the very next verse, this is recorded:

> *When Adam had lived one hundred and thirty years,*
> *he became the father of a son in his own likeness,*
> *according to his image, and named him Seth.*

Notice the difference? The dad had originally been created in God's likeness, but when Seth came along, he was in Adam's likeness—"according to his (his father's) image." Why? Sin had invaded. Genesis 3 tells the grim story. And with the invasion of sin came all its horrible consequences, not the least of which was the beginning of strife, both internal (the root) and external (the fruit).

The disease impacted everything and everyone. Conflict replaced harmony. War replaced peace. Sorrow replaced joy. And things like disobedience, rebellion, argumentation, and even murder became the status quo. In nations. In cities. And in homes as well. Yes, marriages were not exempt. Unlike the original match, husbands and wives became selfish, demanding, brutal, unfaithful, angry, hateful, and competitive.

The nation Israel, God's chosen people, ultimately began to lose their distinction. They ignored God's directions and intermarried with foreigners—non-Israelites. The Jew-Gentile mixture was more than God would allow . . . so a compromise was provided by Moses. A "certificate of divorce" (Deuteronomy 24:1-4) was permitted due to the rampant epidemic that was threatening the uniqueness of Israel. Because of the stubborn, rebellious will of sinful people—Jesus called it "hardness of heart"—divorce evolved. But remember, it was not desired or designed in God's original arrangement for marriage. Sin polluted the plan.

Let's see if I can illustrate the problem another way. Pretend you and your family save enough money to buy a swimming pool. You meet with a builder and you discuss your design preferences. He smiles as he watches you sign the contract and give him your first check. The hole is dug, the reinforcement steel is installed, the cement is blown in, the plaster and tile are finished, and everybody is ecstatic. He kept his word and you paid the bill. Now, of course, the water

needs to be added. As the pool begins to fill up, a strange color   139
appears before your eyes—Green. Not crystal clear . . . not even
bright blue. No, it's green. And the longer you watch, the
greener it gets!

Now, you never intended to have green water. You en-
visioned a sparkling, clear, inviting pool . . . that was your
original plan. But an enemy has come without invitation.
Germs. And the longer that enemy stays, uncontested, the
more putrid the pool appears. So you must make a concession. A compromise is essential, unless you choose to fill up
the pool with dirt and forget all about swimming. You must
add chemicals. Chlorine and acid and other materials must
be placed into your lovely, once-white-and-ideal pool. They
will burn your eyes and bleach your swimsuit . . . but if you're
going to have a pool at all, chemicals must be used to counteract the germs. Like it or not (and you don't), you must compromise with the original plan.

And so it is with marriage. Because of the harsh presence
and consequences of sin, divorce was permitted, lest
marriage and the distinctives of a home that modeled
Jehovah's character be completely nullified and destroyed. In
that sense, divorce became a way of salvaging the believer's
distinctives. But remember—it was never God's original
intention or desire. It was permitted once the ravages of
sinfulness reached threatening proportions.

When Is It Acceptable To Remarry?

Enough of history. Let's come to the
present. The question everyone wants answered is this: When
is divorce permissible? Because of limited time and space, I
will spare you a lot of verbiage and supportive quotations.
Suffice it to say, I will answer the question with remarriage in
mind. In other words, my answers assume that we are really
asking, "Are there any biblical grounds for remarriage?"

I believe there are. I have searched the Scriptures, read
everything I can get my hands on, and discussed this issue
with my wife, my friends, fellow staff, and church board
members, pastors, many theological professors, and other
serious students of the Bible. I have talked with numerous
divorced people, single persons, married couples, publishers,
authors on the subject, and authorities in the field—both

140 Christian and non-Christian. Here are my conclusions, simplified for the sake of clarity.

I believe the Christian has biblical grounds for remarriage when the divorce transpired under one of the three situations described in the following pages.

A Marriage and Divorce Prior to Salvation

1. *When the marriage and divorce occurred prior to salvation.*

In 2 Corinthians 5:17 we read these words:

> *Therefore if any man is in Christ, he is a new creature; the old things passed away; behold, new things have come.*

I take this literally. I even take it to the extreme! I think "new" means "new". . . . So when God promises the believing sinner that He is "a new creature," then I take that to mean exactly that. A brand new, fresh creation. Unlike before.

> The Greek term, *kainos*, means . . . "that which is unaccustomed or unused, not new in time, recent, but new as to form or quality, of different nature from what is contrasted as old."[1]

"Fresh" would be an acceptable synonym. It is used in the New Testament to describe Christ's "new commandment" to His disciples (John 13:34), the "new covenant" (Matthew 26:28-29), the sinner being made a "new man" (Ephesians 2:15), having a "new self" (Ephesians 4:24), our being given a "new name" in heaven (Revelation 2:17), and the "new heaven and a new earth" John the apostle saw (Revelation 21:1).

There can be no question about it, this has in mind the brand new, fresh, unused creature one becomes at the moment of salvation. And if that isn't enough, Paul goes on to add "the old things passed away" at that same time. Again, I take that literally. The old life, with all its old characteristics and sins. They are, in grace, removed. The best word is *forgiven.* Totally and completely.

If that seems too extreme for you, perhaps it would help to read, slowly, those opening words in Ephesians 2:

> *And you were dead in your trespasses and sins,*
> *in which you formerly walked according to the course*
> *of this world, according to the prince of the power of*
> *the air, of the spirit that is now working in the sons*
> *of disobedience.*
> *Among them we too all formerly lived in the lusts of*
> *our flesh, indulging the desires of the flesh and of*
> *the mind, and were by nature children of wrath,*
> *even as the rest.*
>
> *But God, being rich in mercy, because of His great*
> *love with which He loved us,*
> *even when we were dead in our transgressions,*
> *made us alive together with Christ (by grace you have*
> *been saved),*
> *and raised us up with Him, and seated us with Him*
> *in the heavenly places, in Christ Jesus,*
> *in order that in the ages to come He might show the*
> *surpassing riches of His grace in kindness toward us*
> *in Christ Jesus* (vv. 1-7).

and just a few verses later in the same chapter:

> *So then you are no longer strangers and aliens,*
> *but you are fellow citizens with the saints, and are of*
> *God's household,*
> *having been built upon the foundation of the apostles*
> *and prophets, Christ Jesus Himself being the corner*
> *stone,*
> *in whom the whole building, being fitted together*
> *is growing into a holy temple in the Lord;*
> *in whom you also are being built together into a*
> *dwelling of God in the Spirit* (vv. 19-22).

Quite frankly, it is beyond my comprehension that passages such as these (there are dozens more) exclude divorce. If they do, then divorce is the only sin not covered by the blood of Christ. It is the one, permanent spot in our past that cannot be washed away. Furthermore, it is then questionable that we can take the words of David at face value when he writes:

> *He has not dealt with us according to our sins,*
> *Nor rewarded us according to our iniquities.*
> *For as high as the heavens are above the earth,*

142

> So great is His lovingkindness toward those who
> fear Him.
>   As far as the east is from the west,
> So far has He removed our transgressions from us
> (Psalm 103:10-12).

No, I believe "new" means "new." And when God promises the passing away of "old things," it surely includes divorce prior to salvation. After all, being alienated from God and at enmity with Him, how could any unbeliever possibly know His will regarding the choice of a lifetime mate? Having thought through this very carefully, I believe it falls within the context of God's superabundant grace to wipe our slate clean when we turn, by faith, to Christ the Lord.

When the marriage and divorce occurred prior to salvation, I believe God grants His "new creation" the freedom to re-marry.

An Immoral and Unrepentant Partner

2. *When one's mate is guilty of sexual immorality and is unwilling to repent and live faithfully with the marriage partner.*

Much has been written on this particular issue, I realize. I repeat, I have read everything I can get my hands on, so I do not write these words hurriedly or superficially. I am fully aware of the difficulties connected with determining who is really the guilty party when it comes to sexual promiscuity. I also acknowledge the subjectivity involved in identifying "sexual immorality." Such matters must be carefully determined, usually with the help of a qualified counselor who can provide objectivity and wisdom in matters this serious. Each case *must* be considered independently.

Nevertheless, we cannot ignore or deny what Christ said in Matthew 19:9:

> "And I say to you, whoever divorces his wife,
> except for immorality, and marries another woman
> commits adultery."

All sorts of interpretations have been suggested to explain what our Lord was saying. Frankly, having examined every one of the suggestions and theories (some of them are incred-

ibly forced and complicated), I return to the verse and accept it   143
at face value.

Throughout my Christian life I have operated under a very simple—yet reliable—principle of interpretation:

If the normal sense makes good sense,
seek no other sense.

Let's do that here. Jesus is answering a question (it's in verse 3) asked by some Pharisees. It's a question related to divorce:

"Is it lawful for a man to divorce his wife
for any cause at all?"

This leads to a second question (v. 7) having to do with the reason divorce was permitted in the first place:

"Why then did Moses command to give her a
certificate and divorce her?"

His answer is clear:

He said to them, "Because of your hardness of heart,
Moses permitted you to divorce your wives; but from
the beginning it has not been this way.

And then, to clarify the matter even further, He adds:

"And I say to you, whoever divorces his wife,
except for immorality, and marries another woman
commits adultery."

This is Christ's personal counsel regarding justification for divorce and remarriage. That is the "normal sense" of the verse, hence we need not seek any other sense. The only thing that might help is to understand the meaning of the original term translated "immorality."

It is the Greek word *porneia*, from which we get the term "pornography." Throughout the New Testament it is used repeatedly as a term to describe illicit sexual activity. In the case of married partners, it would refer to intimate sexual involvement with someone other than one's mate—someone either of the opposite (heterosexual infidelity) or of the same sex (homosexual activity).

144   Our Lord has reaffirmed that in the beginning (Adam and Eve in the Garden of Eden), divorce was not present. But due to the "hardness of heart" permission was granted to allow divorce. Jesus spells out in detail when such a divorce and remarriage would be acceptable. When a spouse is guilty of immoral sexual conduct with another person and is unwilling to remain faithful to the innocent partner, the option is there for the faithful mate to divorce and remarry.

Before moving on to the third reason, let me ask you to re-read that last sentence. I want to amplify it for a few moments. Two thoughts need to be emphasized. First, this is not simply a case of quickie sex on the sly—a one-time-only experience. This is *porneia*. I take this to mean an immorality that sug-gests a sustained unwillingness to remain faithful. I hesitate to use the term lest I be misinterpreted—but I think of the idea of an immoral *life style*, an obvious determination to practice a promiscuous relationship outside the bonds of marriage.

Second, the faithful mate has the *option* to leave . . . but such is not mandatory. I have seen numerous marriages re-built rather than ended because the faithful partner had no inner peace pursuing a divorce. How much better to look for ways to make the marriage work rather than anxiously antici-pate evidence that is needed to break off the relationship. But there are occasions when every attempt has been made to keep the marriage together . . . but sustained sexual infidelity won't allow it. It is in such cases our Lord grants freedom from that miserable and unbearable bond.

Desertion By An Unbeliever

3. *When one of the mates is an unbeliever and willfully and permanently deserts the believing part-ner.*

In order for us to understand this, we need to read I Corin-thians 7:12-15 very carefully.

> But to the rest I say, not the Lord, that if any brother
> [a Christian] has a wife who is an unbeliever
> [a non-Christian], and she consents to live with him,
> let him not send her away.
> And a woman [a Christian] who has an unbelieving
> husband [a non-Christian], and he consents to live with
> her, let her not send her husband away.

*For the unbelieving husband is sanctified through
his wife, and the unbelieving wife is sanctified through
her believing husband; for otherwise your children
are unclean, but now they are holy.*

Yet if the unbelieving one [a non-Christian] *leaves,
let him leave; the brother or the sister* [a Christian]
*is not under bondage in such cases, but God has called
us to peace* [brackets mine].

Paul is giving sound advice on marriage. He is offering
counsel nowhere else revealed in Scripture. This passage is
unique in that it addresses the very common problem of a
mixed marriage, i.e., one partner is a Christian, the other is
not. Interestingly, the counsel does not assume that such
marriages are always unbearable. On the contrary, there are
times when harmony and compatibility (to an extent) are possible. In such cases the Christian is strictly forbidden to walk
away from the marriage. If the unbeliever desires to remain —
stay put!

But there are occasions when "the unbelieving one leaves."
Please take note that he or she is not forced out. No, the non-
Christian mate willfully deserts, walks out, refuses to stay,
chooses to leave. What's God's counsel to the Christian who is
left? ". . . let him leave." In other words, the Christian is not
under obligation to plead, to beg, to bargain, or to force the
non-Christian partner to remain. Rather, ". . . let him leave."

But that is not the end of this counsel. Verse 15 goes on to
say:

*. . . the brother or sister is not under bondage in
such cases. . . .*

Of course, the key phrase is "not under bondage." Its
meaning? Well, at the root of the Greek term is *doulos,* the
New Testament term for "slave." Slaves were bound to their
masters, inseparably linked to them. It is a strong word suggesting a firm, solid tie. I'm reminded of the verse in Genesis 2
that says the man "cleaves" to his wife. Remember, that word
means "glue." Paul clearly has the marriage bond in mind
here. Later in the chapter, he refers to this bond as being ter-
minated at the death of one's mate:

146
> A wife is **bound** as long as her husband lives;
> but if her husband is dead, she is free to be married...
> [emphasis mine] (I Corinthians 7:39).

That verse clearly states that death frees us from the "bondage" of marriage, allowing the freedom of remarriage.

It is the term "bound" that interests us. Back in verse 15 we are told that the deserted Christian is *not* in bondage any longer. The normal sense of that term is clear. There is no need to seek some other sense. Being free of that "bondage" obviously means being free of the responsibility of that marriage. The desertion of the unsaved partner breaks the bond, thus freeing the believer to divorce and remarry.

Kenneth Wuest's *Expanded Translation* handles the thought quite capably:

> A [Christian] *brother or* [Christian] *sister is not in the position of a slave, namely, bound to the unbelieving husband or unbelieving wife in an indissoluble union in cases such as these; but God has called us* [to live] *in peace."*[2]

You probably don't need to be told that all sorts of suggestions have been made by sincere and qualified students of Scripture to explain what constitutes desertion . . . and to spell out what "not under bondage" really means. Because I promised to spare you numerous quotations and tedious pages of verbiage, I'll not attempt to represent all the opinions that range from unbelievably conservative to downright crazy (in my opinion!). But perhaps a word of caution is needed.

When we read of the departure of the unbelieving partner, obviously Paul is not referring to a temporary, quick decision to chuck it all and bail out . . . only to return in a little while. No, leaving means leaving. Permanence is definitely in mind. It implies a determined and willful decision that results in leaving the relationship with no desire to return, no interest in cultivating that home, no plan to bear the responsibilities, and no commitment to the vows once taken. That's "leaving." And the one being left has little doubt in such cases. The marriage is over. Finished. Ended.

It was in just such a case I became involved many, many years ago. The wife and mother of three (a Christian) was literally "left" by her husband, who happened to be a medical doctor. The man, an unbeliever, would no longer tolerate her relationship to Jesus Christ, even though she was exceedingly careful not to cram it down his throat. In fact, she remained a charming, affectionate, and gracious mate in spite of his obnoxious actions and cruel remarks. Ultimately, however, he walked away. No provision was made to help her financially or otherwise. Embarrassed and heartsick, *his* parents stepped in and generously assisted their daughter-in-law for an extended period of time. Still . . . no word from her husband. He had definitely left. She remained faithful, but he was now gone.

A divorce followed. The woman walked with God through the whole painful experience. She was a remarkable model of patience and forgiveness. Bitterness never crept in. The marriage had ended, but by no means was her life finished.

Through a chain of events too lengthy to describe, she met the man who had been her high school sweetheart. He had never married, for in some strange way he was convinced the Lord would one day bring the two of them together. Although he had lost track of her whereabouts, he had this internal confidence they would someday marry. By the way, he was also a medical doctor . . . and had come to know Christ personally. Their courtship was beautiful to behold.

I had the privilege of officiating at the ceremony—an unforgettable delight. Just last year my wife and I saw them at a large Christian gathering. Their marriage is more solid than ever. Both are spiritually on target. And their family, now grown, is a close, harmonious unit of deep and meaningful affection. Even though her unbelieving mate had left, God kept His hand on her life. He came to her rescue and met her need. In grace. In abundance.

A Summary and a Warning

I agree with John R. W. Stott:

[Divorce was] *a divine concession to human weakness.*[3] No Christian should aggressively seek the dissolution of his or her marriage bond. Some of the very best things God has to

148   teach His children are learned while working through marital difficulties. Endless stories could be told of how God honored the perseverance of abused and ignored partners as they refused to give up.

But in certain extreme cases, against the wishes and efforts of the committed mate, the marriage bond is destroyed beyond any human ability to restore it. Scripture teaches that God's "divine concession to human weakness" is occasionally justified, allowing the Christian divorced person the right and freedom to remarry in the Lord. There are three such cases set forth in God's Word, each provided by His grace:

- First, when the marriage and divorce occurred prior to salvation (2 Corinthians 5:17).

- Second, when one's mate is guilty of sexual immorality and is unwilling to repent and live faithfully with the marriage partner (Matthew 19:9).

- Third, when one of the mates is an unbeliever and willfully and permanently deserts the believing partner (1 Corinthians 7:15).

Before closing the chapter, a warning must be sounded. Being human and sinful and weak, we are all equipped with a remarkable ability to rationalize. Unless we consciously guard against it, when we experience marital difficulties, we'll begin to search for a way *out* instead of a way *through*. Given sufficient time in the crucible, divorce will seem our only option, our long-awaited and much-deserved utopia. And we will begin to push in that direction, at times ignoring the inner voice of God's Spirit and at other times violating the written principles of God's Word. Either is a grievous act.

I warn all of us against such thought and actions. To carry out that carnal procedure is to short-circuit the better plan God has arranged for His people and, worse than that, is to twist the glorious grace of God into a guilt-relieving excuse for giving us what we have devised instead of accepting what He has designed.

Where God permits divorce and remarriage, humbly let us accept it without fear or guilt. Let us not call "unclean" what He now calls clean. But neither let us put words in His mouth and make Him say what He, in fact, has not said. No matter how miserable we may be.

There is something much worse than living with a mate in disharmony. It's living with God in disobedience.

[1] W. E. Vine, *Expository Dictionary of New Testament Words*, 4 vols. (Old Tappan, New Jersey: Fleming H. Revell Company, 1940), 3:109.

[2] Kenneth S. Wuest, *The New Testament, An Expanded Translation* (Grand Rapids: William B. Eerdmans Publishing Company, 1961), p. 394.

[3] John R. W. Stott, *Christian Counter-Culture* (Downers Grove, IL.: InterVarsity Press, 1978), p. 95.

10

COMMITMENT IS THE KEY

The 1980 Winter Olympics ended yesterday. As I write these words, Monday-morning sports pages all across America contain similar headlines to the *Los Angeles Times*.[1]

"THE AMERICAN DREAM TURNS TO GOLD"

A phenomenon has occurred. A bunch of no-name college kids and minor-league rejects have whipped the cream of international hockey—the Soviets, who had not lost an Olympic hockey game in *12 years* . . . who have been wearing gold medals since 1964!

No longer. A group of kids (all in their teens and early 20s) have startled the athletic world. Everyone except a coach named Herb Brooks and this gang of hot dogs on skates said it couldn't be done. It was a silly, unattainable, impossible dream two weeks ago. Unlike the predictions of experts regarding speed skater Eric Heiden, who won five gold medals and emerged as the Olympic superstar, nobody gave this improbable little hockey team a second glance.

How did they do it? Honestly, now—what turned the American dream to gold? How was it possible for them to tie the

152 Swedes, clobber the Czechs, beat the Russians, and come from behind to whip the Finns 4-2 for the final victory?

Well, if you are expecting a super-duper secret, you know, some hidden-surprise play they used, you obviously didn't watch the games. Those confident kids from the Midwest and East didn't rely on rabbit-in-the-hat tricks to win. They faced veteran finesse teams, one after another, with a game plan as old as hockey itself: Never back down, never quit, hang tough, keep hammering away, stay at it, regardless.

In a word: *commitment.*

In our permissive, irresponsible, escapism mentality, commitment is almost a dirty word. Those who would rather rationalize and run than stick with it and watch God pull off a miracle or two (not to mention shaping us in the process) resist this whole concept. If you, personally, are a runner, you are not going to like this chapter.

A Vow Is A Vow

Marriage isn't begun in a context of vagueness and uncertainty. Two people, fully conscious and very much awake and aware, declare their vows. I realize vows may vary, but without exception, they include words like:

". . . for better or for worse . . ."
and

". . . 'til death do us part."

Right? Remember those words you promised before God? Did He hear you? I'm being facetious—*of course He heard you!* Does He take such vows seriously? Read for yourself:

*When you make a vow to God, do not be late in
paying it, for He takes no delight in fools. Pay what
you vow!* (Ecclesiastes 5:4).

Yes, He not only takes them seriously, He remembers them permanently. A vow is a vow. A solemn promise by which one individual binds himself/herself to an act or service or another person. What is it God commands?

"Pay what you vow!"

We are to fear God. He says so. We are to keep our word.

Now, listen very carefully. Read this slowly. No amount of psychological therapy, positive thinking (often dubbed "grace"), semantic footwork with the biblical text, alternative concepts, or mutual support from family and friends can remove your responsibility to *keep your vow.* Unless you are a victim of the conditions I stated in the previous chapter (biblical bases for divorce and remarriage), you are responsible for your marriage vow. I repeat—a vow is a vow.

Of course it's difficult! For sure, there will be times you are inwardly convinced you can't go on. But I remind you of your vow, your stated commitment:

"*. . . for better, for worse. . . .*"

What you are experiencing may be some of the "worse." And no marriage is exempt from such times.

The other day I drove over to some friends' house to pick up their daughter so she could go ice-skating with one of my children. The mom and dad were hanging wallpaper together. Now . . . if you've ever done that as a husband-wife team, you know how tough that project is on a marriage. He and I laughed together as I shared with him the three stages couples go through when they hang wallpaper together:

First week: The couple considers separation.
Second week: The couple separates.
Third week: Divorce proceedings begin!

After the joke, he leaned over to me in the car and said something I wish I could hear every Christian husband and wife declare. With great sincerity, he stated these words:

"Chuck, do you know what makes our marriage work?
One word: commitment. I am committed to that woman
and she is to me—forever."

May his tribe increase.

Why So Little Commitment?

What's happening? Why is the divorce rate skyrocketing? How come so many Christians are walking away from their commitment with no biblical justification?

I have boiled it down to four reasons. Perhaps there are many more, but these are the four I encounter most often.

154 Public Opinion

Ours is the "everybody's doin' it" craze. You know, the "don't sweat it" philosophy. The media ignores or, with a slick wave of the hand, glosses over the fact that a certain person recently walked away from his or her marriage. So does the press. If a person's books are doing well, who really wants to make waves about the author's private life?

All this dulls the senses of the public. The edge of our discernment is dulled. By and by we tend to tolerate (and later *embrace*) the same compromise. No longer is it in vogue to be ashamed or embarrassed—certainly not to blush! Guilt is now an obscene term, something no one should bring on another by asking the hard questions. Public opinion okays actions—and thereby they stand approved.

This is nothing new. In Deuteronomy 6 God's people, the Hebrews, are just about to enter a vast, new territory. The promised land. Canaanite country. Sounds inviting, but it held numerous perils for those monotheistic, protected, sheltered people who had hovered around a cloud by day and a fire by night. Idolatry, humanism, and carnality in the raw awaited them in Canaan. And they would soon be living in that pagan culture where public opinion would be in conflict with their training under Moses. So God prepares them with this strong warning:

"Then it shall come about when the Lord your God brings you into the land which He swore to your fathers, Abraham, Isaac and Jacob, to give you, great and splendid cities which you did not build,

and houses full of all good things which you did not fill, and hewn cisterns which you did not dig, vineyards and olive trees which you did not plant, and you shall eat and be satisfied,

then watch yourself, lest you forget the Lord who brought you from the land of Egypt, out of the house of slavery.

"You shall fear only the Lord your God; and you shall worship Him, and swear by His name.

"You shall not follow other gods, any of the gods of the peoples who surround you,

for the Lord your God in the midst of you is a jealous God; . . ." (Deuteronomy 6:10-15a).

Without question, the Lord God stood against His people being dulled and lulled to sleep by the people who surrounded them. How relevant! Public opinion has a way of weakening our commitment.

Accommodating Theology

There is another reason Christian marriages are weaker in commitment. I call it "accommodating theology." This is nothing more than fitting the Bible into my life style. In other words, I alter my theology instead of adjusting my life. My experiential tail wags the biblical dog.

Ezekiel the prophet faced a group of people who did this. Jehovah warned him ahead of time so it wouldn't jolt him too severely. Read Ezekiel 33:30-33:

> *"But as for you, son of man, your fellow citizens who talk about you by the walls and in the doorways of the houses, speak to one another, each to his brother, saying, 'Come now, and hear what the message is which comes forth from the Lord.'*
> *"And they come to you as people come, and sit before you as My people, and hear your words, but they do not do them, for they do the lustful desires expressed by their mouth, and their heart goes after their gain.*
> *"And behold, you are to them like a sensual song by one who has a beautiful voice and plays well on an instrument; for they hear your words, but they do not practice them.*
> *"So when it comes to pass—as surely it will—then they will know that a prophet has been in their midst.*

The Living Bible says it straight:

> *"They hear what you say, but don't pay any attention to it"* (v. 32b).

Now, don't misunderstand. They are not obnoxious and ugly. No. In fact, they are gracious, flattering, and even good at listening. But down underneath, they *really* have no plans whatsoever to let biblical theology get in their way.

This requires great rationalization. It demands the ability to ignore some obvious things, reinterpret and explain away certain passages of Scripture, and to call upon grace (that

156 vast dumping ground for every conceivable act of disobedience) to get them through. By accommodating one's theology, it is remarkable what the mind can do to remove even the slightest trace of guilt! And by the way, it really helps to find an author or two to verify such accommodations.

I write with emotion. I'm sure it shows through. Within the past three years I have watched about ten marriages dissolve. All Christian marriages. Yes, both husbands and wives. All very much involved in Christian activities and church ministries. In each case one of the mates in each marriage has willfully (and skillfully) accommodated his or her theology so that the Scriptures actually "approved" their plans to walk out.

There were no ugly fights or bold public announcements like, "I am denying the faith!" No need for that. Calmly and with reserved respectability, they simply left. That's it. Against my counsel and strong efforts to stop them. Against scriptural injunctions. Against their mates' desires. In spite of the certain damage to their children. And regardless of the shame it brought against the name of God and the Church of Jesus Christ.

Hang on—not one seems to be wrestling with much guilt or personal shame. In fact, several say they have never been happier. A few openly insist they are closer to the Lord than ever before in their lives. Some are still engaged in public ministries.

How? Accommodating theology, that's how. The enemy wins many a victory by this means.

Delayed Consequences

A third reason we see less commitment and an increasing number of broken marriages is a practical one—they get away with it without divine judgment.

Solomon once wrote about this:

> Because the sentence against an evil deed
> is not executed quickly, therefore the hearts of the sons
> of men among them are given fully to do evil
> (Ecclesiastes 8:11).

The Living Bible simplifies the verse:

Because God does not punish sinners instantly,
people feel it is safe to do wrong.

You've heard it before: "All God's accounts are not settled this month." I remember reading the words of a sixteenth-century saint similar to that one:

"God does not pay at the end of every day.
But at the end, He pays."[2]

I'll be honest. This is one of the most difficult things for me to accept. It's beyond me why a holy and just God does not deal more quickly with disobedience among His wayward children. It would certainly do a lot to build a wholesome fear in the lives of those being tempted to disobey. But even though I cannot explain it, I must declare it: Delayed consequences cause couples to walk away from each other.

Funny, isn't it? Being here-and-now thinkers, we tend to deny the devastating effects divorce will ultimately have on us and, for sure, on our children. Because momentary relief is such a determined pursuit by an unhappy mate, the added "benefit" of little or no divine discipline provides the encouragement needed to carry out the plan.

But the Bible clearly teaches that wrong will not ultimately win out. God never smiles on disobedience. At the end, let it be understood, He pays.

Christian Approval
There is a fourth reason so many believers are breaking the bond of marriage. It ties in with the third one we just considered. For lack of a better way to say it, Christian approval encourages it.

Remember the Corinthian church? Remember how lax they were with the brother in their midst who was living in sin? Listen to the account:

It is actually reported that there is immorality
among you, and immorality of such a kind as does not
exist even among the Gentiles, that someone has his
father's wife.

158
> *And you have become arrogant, and have not mourned instead, in order that the one who had done this deed might be removed from your midst.*
>
> *For I, on my part, though absent in body but present in spirit, have already judged him who has so committed this, as though I were present.*
>
> *In the name of our Lord Jesus, when you are assembled, and I with you in spirit, with the power of our Lord Jesus,*
>
> *I have decided to deliver such a one to Satan for the destruction of his flesh, that his spirit may be saved in the day of the Lord Jesus.*
>
> *Your boasting is not good. Do you not know that a little leaven leavens the whole lump of dough?*
>
> *Clean out the old leaven, that you may be a new lump, just as you are in fact unleavened. For Christ our Passover also has been sacrificed* (1 Corinthians 5:1-7).

Church discipline is virtually unheard of in our day. The Corinthians were equally guilty of that same problem. They had a man who was guilty of incest. Rather than being ashamed, rather than applying discipline, they boasted about their tolerance and they were proud of how broadminded they had become.

And so it is in America today. Precious few are the churches that take a stand against disobedience in their midst. How seldom do we hear of someone being disciplined because he or she breaks his marital vow! Such Christian approval has helped foster a shallow view of commitment in our day.

A Needed Clarification

It would be wise for us to pause a moment and clarify a matter seldom addressed in books on marriage, especially those that support commitment to the vows that were taken. There are unique occasions when it may be necessary for some couples to separate, temporarily. Due to various circumstances—all of them prompted either by emotional sickness or gross demonstrations of sin to the point of danger—there are times when life and health are seriously threatened. To remain together in such cases frequently leads to permanent damage and even tragedy in a home.

It is unrealistic and unfair to think that regardless of sure danger and possible loss of life, a godly mate and helpless children should subject themselves to brutality and other forms of extreme mistreatment. *At that point, commitment to Christ supersedes all other principles in a home.* I am not advocating divorce . . . but I do suggest restraint and safety via a separation.

It is one thing to be in subjection. It is another thing entirely to become the brunt of indignity, physical assault, sexual perversion, and uncontrolled rage. Since the believer's body is the temple of God's Spirit, it is *unthinkable* that He is pleased to have our bodies mauled and mistreated by sick and/or thoughtless mates who care little about their family's welfare and think of nothing but their own twisted gratification.

At such crisis times, call for help! Seek out a Christian friend who can assist you. Talk with your pastor or a competent counselor who will provide both biblical guidance and emotional support. And pray! Pray that your Lord will bring about changes in the unbearable circumstances surrounding you. Ask for deliverance, safety, stability, and great grace to see you through, to settle your fears, to calm your spirit so you can think and act responsibly.

What is it David writes?

> *Be gracious, O God, for man has trampled upon me;*
> *Fighting all day long he oppresses me,*
> *My foes have trampled upon me all day long,*
> *For they are many who fight proudly against me.*
> *When I am afraid, I will put my trust in Thee.*
> *In God, whose word I praise,*
> *In God I have put my trust;*
> *I shall not be afraid. What can mere man do to me?*
> *All day long they distort my words;*
> *All their thoughts are against me for evil.*
> *They attack, they lurk,*
> *They watch my steps,*
> *As they have waited to take my life. . . .*
> *Then my enemies will turn back in the day*
> *when I call;*
> *This I know, that God is for me.*

160
> *In God, whose word I praise,*
> *In the Lord, whose word I praise,*
> *In God I have put my trust, I shall not be afraid.*
> *What can man do to me?* (Psalm 56:1-6, 9-11).

Powerful words, waiting to be claimed!

Principles That Enhance Commitment

So far, much of what I have been writing has been more negative than positive. As I near the end of this chapter, I want to turn that emphasis in another direction. Let's consider several principles from 1 Corinthians 7 that enhance our marital commitment. To help make these thoughts stick, I will be brief and to the point. I find four principles in this great chapter.

No Conflict Is Unsolvable

1. Christian marriages have conflicts, but they are not beyond solution.

Take a look at 1 Corinthians 7:28:

> *But if you should marry, you have not sinned; and if a virgin should marry, she has not sinned. Yet such will have trouble in this life, and I am trying to spare you.*

Writing with a compassionate heart, Paul says that he is trying to "spare us." One of his suggestions is that some not even marry (vv. 7, 26). But this is not God's will for most of us. So then, when we marry, we can be sure of this—times of disagreement, fleshly flare-ups, are bound to happen.

Remember this: There is no such thing as a home completely without conflicts. The last couple to live "happily ever after" was Snow White and Prince Charming. Even though you are committed to your mate, there will still be times of tension, tears, struggle, disagreement, and impatience. Commitment doesn't erase our humanity! That's bad news, but it's realistic.

The good news is this: With the Lord Jesus Christ living within you and with His Book, the Bible, waiting to be called upon for counsel and advice, *no conflict is beyond solution.*

Before moving on to the next principle, drop down to verses 32 through 35:

But I want you to be free from concern. One who is unmarried is concerned about the things of the Lord, how he may please the Lord;

but one who is married is concerned about the things of the world, how he may please his wife,

and his interests are divided. And the woman who is unmarried, and the virgin, is concerned about the things of the Lord, that she may be holy both in body and spirit; but one who is married is concerned about the things of the world, how she may please her husband.

And this I say for your own benefit; not to put a restraint upon you, but to promote what is seemly, and to secure undistracted devotion to the Lord.

Talk about realism! If you are married, there is no such thing as giving the Lord your "undistracted devotion" 100 percent of the time. Know why? Because you married a *distraction!* Just the difference between you and your mate—the male-female differences—have a way of keeping you trusting.

In our day of unisex and narrowing the gap between men and women, it is easy to pick up an erroneous idea that you and your partner are very much alike. No, that simply isn't true. Listen to one authority:

An effort has been underway for the past few years to prove that men and women are identical, except for the ability to bear children. Radical feminists have vigorously (and foolishly) asserted that the only distinction between the sexes is culturally and environmentally produced. Nothing could be farther from the truth; males and females differ biochemically, anatomically, and emotionally. In truth, they are unique in every cell of their bodies, for men carry a different chromosomal pattern than women. There is also considerable evidence to indicate that the hypothalamic region, located just above the pituitary gland in the mid-brain, is "wired" very uniquely for each of the sexes. Thus, the hypothalamus (known as the seat of the emotions) provides women with a different psychological frame of reference than that of men. Further, female sexual desire tends to be

somewhat cyclical, correlated with the menstrual
calendar, whereas males are acyclical. These and
other features account for the undeniable fact that
masculine and feminine expressions of sexuality are
far from identical. Failure to understand this
uniqueness can produce a continual source of marital
frustration and guilt.[3]

And never forget, those differences create conflicts . . . but in the Lord and under His control, none are unsolvable.

Persistence Pays Off

2. Working through is harder than walking out, but it is God's way.

Again, listen to several verses from 1 Corinthians 7:

Are you bound to a wife? Do not seek to be released.
Are you released from a wife? Do not seek a wife (v. 27).

Brethren, let each man remain with God in that
condition in which he was called (v. 24).

But to the married I give instructions, not I, but the
Lord, that the wife should not leave her husband
(but if she does leave, let her remain unmarried, or
else be reconciled to her husband), and that the
husband should not send his wife away.
But to the rest I say, not the Lord, that if any brother
has a wife who is an unbeliever, and she consents
to live with him, let him not send her away.
And a woman who has an unbelieving husband,
and he consents to live with her, let her not send her
husband away (vv. 10-13).

The obvious, underlying theme here is like our Olympic hockey team's game plan: Don't quit, hang tough, stay at it, regardless.

My wife and I declare our commitment to each other several times a year. We get alone, often for an overnight somewhere cozy and private. While there we look at each other and *verbalize* our promise to remain faithful. We actually declare aloud our commitment. Can't explain how or why it works, but there's something reassuring about putting things like that into words. As our ears hear what our mouths are saying (from our hearts, actually), our loyalty is reaffirmed.

Another fact is this: We have removed the term "divorce" from our vocabulary when we are working through a tough time. We do not refer to it, we do not use it as a threat, nor do we tuck it away in a safe place in our minds for some future use. The passages we just read pulsate with commitment:

"Do not seek to be released . . . ."
". . . remain . . . ."
". . . the wife should not leave . . . ."
". . . the husband should not send his wife away."

Why? Why is it best to work through rather than walk out? I can think of several reasons:

- It is the continual counsel of Scripture.

- One's own growth in Christ is strengthened.

- The testimony of Christ before the public is enhanced.

- Working through forces needed changes. To walk out means we take our same hangups into the next relationship.

- Children in the family remain more secure, stable, and balanced. They also learn to run if parents run . . . or work out the difficulties if that's what mom and dad model.

I'm sure there are some who read these words and disagree—especially if you are thinking of walking out. Before you do, let me share with you a brief observation from an article out of a recently released secular magazine:

No Role Models: For better or worse, divorce continues to split families at an alarming rate. The number of children involved in divorce has tripled in the last twenty years. And though parents, children and professionals are struggling to deal with such new domestic realities as single-parent families, there are no long-standing precedents, no established role models to draw from. Divorce and its aftermath can be a labyrinth of confusion and conflict, some of which may never be resolved. [4]

And then, quoting a professional divorce lecturer and author, Rabbi Earl Grollman, who believes divorce can be more traumatic than death,

"The big difference is, death has closure, it's over. With divorce, it's never over." [5]

164   There can be no denying it. Walking out may *seem to be* the solution. Even the secular authorities are beginning to question that now. No, there is a better answer than walking out. Work through!

God Defends Unselfish Commitment

3. Being committed to one's mate is not a matter of *demanding* rights, but *releasing* rights.

Listen to these words:

> *Let the husband fulfill his duty to his wife, and likewise also the wife to her husband.*
> *The wife does not have authority over her own body, but the husband does; and likewise also the husband does not have authority over his own body, but the wife does* (1 Corinthians 7:3-4).

A couple of words in those verses pierce deeply, don't they? Duty. Authority. Selfishness within us *hates* terms like that! "I've got my rights!" says today's liberated woman. "Hey, don't tie me down!" yells today's macho man. No marriage will flourish under that kind of philosophy.

God has a better way: Surrender your rights. Lay down your arms. Release your grip on the things you've been fighting for. Commit the risk to God. Trust Him to defend you and keep you from being ripped off. I say that to husbands just as much as I do wives. Releasing rights, ideally, is a mutual thing—a duet, not a solo.

Commitment Glorifies God

4. The Christian's ultimate goal in life is not to be happy, but to glorify God.

This is one of the greatest insights God ever gave me. If you will meditate on it long enough, deeply enough, it will literally revolutionize your life. It has mine. It is based on the last two verses in 1 Corinthians 6 and leads into these thoughts we've been considering on commitment:

> *Or do you not know that your body is a temple of the Holy Spirit who is in you, whom you have from God, and that you are not your own?*
> *For you have been bought with a price: therefore glorify God in your body* (vv. 19-20).

Two significant thoughts deserve our full attention. I will   165
personalize them:

I AM NOT MY OWN.
I AM TO GLORIFY GOD.

If it were possible to set in concrete one all-encompassing truth from this chapter, those two statements would do it. Please read them again.

Our ultimate goal, our highest calling in life is to glorify God—not to be happy. Let that sink in! Glorifying Him is our greatest pursuit. Not to get our way. Not to be comfortable. Not to find fulfillment. Not even to be loved or to be appreciated or to be taken care of. Now these *are* important, but they are not primary.

As I glorify Him, He sees to it that other essential needs are met . . . or my need for them diminishes. Believe me, this concept will change your entire perspective on yourself, your life, and your marriage.

A Concluding Thought On Commitment

We have thought about several reasons Christian marriages have grown weaker in our generation. We have also given consideration to some principles that strengthen our commitment to our mates. Every major point has been amplified from one or more biblical statements. And yet . . . I'm sure a few of you who read these words look upon your situation as an exception. Frowning, you'll lay this book aside with a sigh and think, "But you just don't know the person I'm married to. Our only answer is divorce. I just can't commit myself to this marriage. We're finished."

For your sake, I share the following letter. It was written to me almost a year after I spoke on commitment in our church in Fullerton, California. The wife who wrote it understands what a difficult marriage is all about. Believe me, I know. Their home seemed beyond repair.

Dear Pastor Chuck:

Tonight, I commented to you about how much I appreciated your comments concerning your stand on divorce, remarriage, and commitment. I thank you for your supportive and compassionate understanding of this area of difficulty in many marriages.

I really wanted to tell you how I have been blessed since I last wrote you nearly ten months ago (after you gave your sermons on commitment). I decided to remain steadfast in commitment to my own marriage that was in the middle of a divorce action at that time. God has changed me. He has given me a new love for my husband and, in turn, my husband has been changing in his attitude toward me. He is still uncommitted about his relationship with Jesus— a miracle I am anticipating.

Six months ago we sat and listened to a psychologist (not a Christian) tell us to get on with the divorce because there was absolutely nothing left of our marriage and no basis upon which to build.

Well, God's grace has allowed the contrary. It's still a real struggle some days, but I have learned that as we "pull" toward each other rather than "push" at each other, the direction is more secure and sound . . . .

So, commitment is not just another word in my vocabulary. It has become a real part of my life.

> *In Him,*
>
> *(signed)*

No, commitment is not just another word. It is *the* watchword for a struggling, hurting, eroding marriage that seems destined to be locked up and closed forever.

Commitment is the key.

---

[1] *Los Angeles Times,* February 25, 1980, Part II, page 1.

[2] Ann of Austria

[3] Dr. James Dobson, *What Wives Wish Their Husbands Knew About Women* (Wheaton, Illinois: Tyndale House Publishers, Inc., 1975), p. 114.

[4] Linda Bird Francke and others, "Children of Divorce," *Newsweek* [New York], February 11, 1980, pp. 58-63.

[5] Ibid., p. 63.

11

DON'T JUST GET OLDER, GET BETTER!

"*Tomorrow we shall meet,*
Death and I—
And he shall thrust his sword
Into one who is wide awake.

But in the meantime how grievous the memory
Of hours frittered away." Dag Hammarskjold[1]

"*Through his sorrow, Kunta was surprised to hear*
that the old gardener had been called 'Josephus.'
He wondered what the gardener's true name had
been—the name of his African forefathers—and to
what tribe they had belonged. He wondered if
the gardener himself had known. Most likely he
had died as he had lived—without ever learning
who he really was." Alex Haley [2]

Growing older is a process from which we cannot escape. As the reality of aging looms larger, strange things occur.

About the time we start making enough money to take care of our family's needs, the kids are grown and gone. About the time we have enough wisdom to pass on to the next generation, nobody cares to listen (except *grandkids*—God bless

168   'em!). And have you noticed how fast the years roll by? About the time your face clears up, your mind gets fuzzy!

And we've all seen the television commercial that shows a husband whispering tenderly into his wife's ear:

"Honey, you're not getting older—you're getting better."

That's quite a compliment, even though it isn't true. *Everybody gets older.* Maybe we don't show our age and maybe we become sweeter with age. But, nevertheless, we do get older. And age brings tendencies that must be controlled. The real question that needs to be answered is: As we get older, how can we get better? Once all the children have left the nest and two people who honeymooned together 25 to 35 years ago are left to "start over," how can they find fulfillment and delight? How can they preserve that young-at-heart relationship during life's "afternoon" years?

There is an enormous resurgence of interest these days in restoring the grand old Victorian homes of yesteryear. In Los Angeles there is a large organization committed to such projects. Ninety-year-old dwellings that have "weathered decades of structural neglect and suffered the slings of deteriorating neighborhoods"[3] are now being handled with great care. Months are invested as skilled craftsmen and proud owners work hard (and spend multiple thousands) to renovate, refinish, restore, and preserve these elegant mansions of the past. As neglect and deterioration are arrested, beauty returns. These places are not just getting older, they are getting better—literally!

God Desires Our Restoration

An understanding and application of God's guidelines for restoring an aging marriage provide sufficient insurance to sustain the remodeled home when this critical time occurs. In the last two chapters of Ecclesiastes, Solomon sets forth several directives each couple must heed if they genuinely desire to "get better" as they grow older.

Growing Old or Growing Up

But first of all, we need to talk about the difference between "growing old" and "growing up." They aren't necessarily the same thing. Growing old requires nothing but

living. Just the passing of time. Growing up requires a great
deal of discipline.

To grow up, you must work on areas of your life that reflect irresponsibility, foolish thinking, and immature behavior. This is true whether you are 15 or 105! Growing old does not necessarily mean we have grown up. We may have to remind a child or teen-ager who's acting irresponsibly, "Grow up. Get with it. Act your age." At times we may need to say the same thing to ourselves, even though we may be in our 50s or 60s or 70s. Immaturity often rears its scowling head when couples realize their children are gone and for the first time since the honeymoon years, they're alone, together.

In his book *Homemade Happiness*, Wayne Dehoney puts his finger on this tender spot:

> *When two parents wave good-bye to their last child, they are entering one of their most critical periods of marital adjustment. Two roads are open to them. They may accept the situation as life's good gift to explore new heights of marital happiness . . . . Or they may travel a road in increasing loneliness, bitterness and neurotic behavior.*[4]

Some people are surprised to learn that thousands of the couples who divorce each year have been married twenty years or more. This tells us that they have grown older, but many of them haven't grown better. They have chosen not to adapt, adjust, and work through this critical period of their marriage.

Insuring Your Aging

In this chapter, I want to sell you some insurance on your home. The premium has no dollar sign, but the price is terribly high. It requires that you grow up. The particulars of the policy are in Ecclesiastes 11 and 12. But we're going to look at the passage backwards—first Chapter 12, then Chapter 11. (Since I'm left-handed, going backwards makes good sense to me.)

In Chapter 12, Solomon has built to the ultimate climax. In unmistakable terms he clearly implies: "You're getting older." But in Chapter 11 he talks about how to live a better life, even though you're getting older. So, our study will go from the ul-

170   timate to how to prepare for the ultimate. Then, we'll find five guidelines for how to stay younger when you grow older.

The Ultimate In Life: Old Age

Chapter 12 of Ecclesiastes is one of the most realistic passages in all the Bible. I love it for its picturesque symbolism and its sometimes humorous subtleties.

> *Remember also your Creator in the days of your youth, before the evil days come and the years draw near when you will say, "I have no delight in them"* (v. 1).

Direct Warning

Notice that the chapter begins with a command: "Remember . . . ." An exclamation point could follow that first word. God wants you and me to remember *Him*. We are to remember the One who made us, and, ideally, remember Him while we are young, and throughout our growing-up years. (And these years never end, for we never become absolutely mature.) Why? Because there is that tendency in later years to look back and say we have no delight in them. Few people are more bitter and lonely today than those who have grown old alone, away from the Lord, and have turned against life. Verse 2 describes their gloom and depression:

> *. . . before the sun, the light, the moon, and the stars are darkened, and clouds return after the rain.*

Here in Southern California, we look toward the mountains after a rainstorm to enjoy the refreshing view. What a fabulous sight! Bright white mountain peaks stand tall as the sky is purged of pollution. But this isn't the picture here. Instead, there is an old person who, in bitterness, has closed himself in, and the clouds, instead of refreshment, bring only one dark storm after another.

Poet Joyce Kilmer wrote a nostalgic poem many years ago, entitled "The House with Nobody in It." The first and final sections tell the story:

> *Whenever I walk to Suffern, along the Erie track I go by a poor old farm house with its shingles broken and black.*
> *I suppose I've passed it a hundred times*

But I always stop for a minute
And look at that house, the tragic house,
The house with nobody in it.

So whenever I go to Suffern,
Along the Erie track,
I never go by that empty house
Without stopping and looking back.
It hurts me to look at the crumbling roof
And the shutters falling apart,
For I can't help thinking the poor old house
Is a house with a broken heart.[5]

Sad and lonely as that scene may be, there is a tragedy worse than that. Much worse! It is the heartbreaking sight of a lonely, empty, crumbling life scarred by bitterness and cynicism. Solomon warns: Watch out! Keep the Lord in full focus!

Old Age Unveiled

And now the ancient king describes old age (v. 3):

In the day that the watchmen of the house
tremble . . . .

That's describing the trembling lips of a person growing much older.

And the mighty men stoop . . . .

That's a picture of bent legs and a lower back stooped over in age.

The grinding ones stand idle because they
are few . . . .

You have gums instead of teeth. Old age robs us of our ivories!

The other day when I was in a grocery store, I saw an older man dumping jars of baby food into his cart. I thought, "Wow, what a super grandfather. He is stocking up on that baby food so his grandkids will never go hungry." With a friendly grin, I walked up to him and said, "You're really taking care of the babies, aren't you?"

172   "What babies?" he mumbled. "These are mine!"

Grocers will tell you that older people often buy as much baby food as the young parents, simply because they can no longer chew. The problem? Their "grinding ones" are idle.

Those who look through windows grow dim. . . .

The "windows" are your eyes. You know the facts: The older you get, the thicker the lens, the smaller the eyes behind it. I know all about that. I wear glasses with such thick lenses that when I get in a pulpit to preach, I have to be careful about looking at the spotlights, or my pupils might start smoking!

The doors on the street are shut as the sound of the grinding mill is low. . . .

Deafness is setting in. You can't hear that grinding mill as well as you used to. Your pet phrase is, "How's that?"

One will arise at the sound of the bird, and all the daughters of song will sing softly.

Insomnia. Here's an older couple who go to bed at 7:30 p.m. and can't understand why they can't sleep until 8:00 the next morning. At about 3 a.m. they wake up because the clock in the living room chimed three times. Light sleeping is part of growing old. Funny, isn't it? Can't hear much during the day, yet everything at night is amplified!

Furthermore, men are afraid of a high place and of terrors on the road.

Here's the problem of phobias. As we grow older we become afraid of high places, closed-in places, long journeys, or big crowds.

In my rebellious teen-age years, our family visited the capitol building in Austin, Texas. The capitol itself is built with a balcony that wraps around an open area. No matter what floor you go up on, you can lean over and see the Lone Star right in the middle of the floor on the first level. The higher you go, the more your stomach turns as you look over.

As Mother and I had just had an argument, my mouth wasn't doing what it should have been. When Mother looked over the balcony, she said, "Oh, it scares me to get this close. It makes me want to jump."

I answered, "Go ahead, I dare you!" Terrible thing to say! **173**
But when you get older and climb higher, you do begin to fear
falling.

Youth knows no such fears. When I was a little kid, I often
tiptoed across a fallen tree over a deep ravine below. That
thing was at least twenty-five feet above the water. I remember
tossing my sack lunch up in the air, catching it, and doing all
sorts of crazy things out on that tree. I just have heart failure
when I think about doing that now. Why? Because I'm now
middle-aged. I'm no longer thirteen or fourteen. When I'm
sixty, perhaps my fears will be even greater. Going on in the
passage—

> *The almond tree blossoms. . . .*

Perhaps that's a picture of graying hair. At a distance an
almond tree in full blossom has a snowy white appearance.

> *The grasshopper drags himself along. . . .*

His joints are stiff and perhaps he knows the crippling grip of
arthritis. It's a picture of a wizened old man who can scarcely
move those stiff limbs along.

> *The caperberry is ineffective. . . .*

Perhaps that would be sexual impotence . . . maybe the loss of
appetite for food. Ultimately, in life, both occur.

> *Remember Him before the silver cord is broken. . . .*

Now it's serious. Here's a stroke which has broken the silver
cord of life.

> *Remember Him . . . before the golden bowl is crushed.*

This is loss of memory. The golden bowl is probably a reference to our brain, which has housed so many facts in a lifetime. But in old age, we lose our memory. We forget names,
places, and where we were. We lose orientation.

> *The pitcher by the well is shattered and the wheel at
> the cistern is crushed.*

Here are heart failure and circulatory problems. Then, in
verse 7, he describes the ultimate:

174   *Then the dust will return to the earth as it was, and
the spirit will return to God who gave it.*

This passage has built to the climax of life—death.

Saddle Oxfords and Varicose Veins

Ecclesiastes 12 reminds everyone who is growing older (but wants to grow better) that he or she should live realistically. The television commercial is a lie. Romantic as it may sound, you may *be* getting better, but you are *also* getting older. To deny that is to act out a fantasy. I don't know of anything more foolish than a 65-year-old man leaving his wife of some forty years to run around with a young chick who's barely twenty. He is trying to say, "I've still got it to together. I don't need that old woman. I'll go with this young one." It's foolish and yet it goes on all the time.

Even sillier is the aging grandmother who dresses like a high school cheerleader, knotty legs and all. Saddle oxfords and varicose veins don't mix. Old age has dignity and beauty until it tries to be a teen-ager. And nobody laughs over these archaic actors any louder than the teens. You've heard them: "Hey, get a load of that one. Look at her." Such people are not bridging the gap, they're *increasing* it.

The very best thing an older person can do is to admit, "I'm getting older. And I have something to offer just like I am." I appreciate this comment by one woman: "The happiest day of my life was when I stopped trying to look twenty years younger than I am and decided to be myself. There's a special beauty God has given my silver hair." That's the best compliment you can pay yourself. Just live with the fact that you are as old as you are. And ask God to keep you alive, charming, and "in touch."

By the way, your children will help you remember. One day I was in the car with our youngest daughter Colleen. She was singing a little ditty she learned at school:

No matter how small a prune may be,
He's always full of wrinkles.
No matter how small a prune may be,
He's always full of wrinkles.
A little prune is like his dad,
But he ain't wrinkled half as bad!

No matter how small a prune may be,
He's always full of wrinkles.

As we pulled in the driveway, she finished the chorus. She got out and slammed the door, looked at me and said, "Don't forget, Dad, I'm the little prune. *You're* the dad." Off she skipped. I looked in the rear view mirror and thought, "Hey, she really ain't wrinkled half as bad." That's right. That's reality. Ugh!

Support For What's Ahead

The husband or wife who fears getting older and less attractive needs support from the other mate. Something tragic takes place in the heart of an individual who feels physical beauty is the only means for keeping a mate. That doesn't mean we should become ugly physically as we grow older. We need to do all we can do, and then stop and let nature take its course.

Facing reality will help prepare you for some of the danger signals of getting old and losing touch. Some of these are poor communication, loss of compatibility, and refusal to discuss and even compromise here and there. Mature people are not stubborn; yet some of the most stubborn people I know are in their sixties or seventies. They just haven't grown up. Mature people may have deep convictions, but they are open, tolerant, kind, and gracious. They have a long fuse, not a short one. Don't say, "That's just the way God made me." God wants to *remake* you. Your old nature makes you like you are. The new nature wants to remake you.

Five Helpful Guidelines

Now, as we hang a close on this chapter, let's notice those guidelines I mentioned earlier. All but the first one are found in the previous chapter, Ecclesiastes 11.

Face Reality

The first guideline for growing old is *live realistically.* I've been talking about this all through the chapter: You're getting older. Now you should ask, "How can I get better? How can I grow up? How can I stay in touch?"

Those hard questions will assist you as you determine to be a realistic person.

176 Enjoy Living By Giving

The second guideline to help you get better as you grow older is *give generously.*

Cast your bread on the surface of the waters, for you will find it after many days. Divide your portion to seven, or even to eight, for you do not know what misfortune may occur on the earth (Ecclesiastes 11:1-2).

Wise words from a wise man, written especially to those of us growing older. What is he saying? Listen to the paraphrase of *The Living Bible:*

Give generously, for your gifts will return to you later. Divide your gifts among many, for in the days ahead, you yourself may need much help.

These two verses are telling those who have a little bit of this world's goods to share some of it and not keep it all to yourself. The happiest old people I know are those who give, and I mean give generously. Don't think that by keeping it now you will enjoy it in the lives of your children later on after you're gone. Enjoy the results of it right now.

But I think the passage goes deeper than money. It includes money, but it's also saying, "Give of yourself. Stay in touch with the mainstream of life. Let the benchmark of your life be generosity. Let it flow. Let it go." It's when we pull back, close our doors, turn off our internal lights, and sit in selfish silence that we shrivel into the most miserable people on earth.

In connection with this, there's a danger when parents hesitate to release their older, unmarried children. They may be twenty-five, thirty, or forty, not married, and in a quandary over their relationship to their parents.

With my own family, I'm preparing for that right now. I was prompted by an excellent book by Charlie Shedd entitled *Promises to Peter* [6] to put down some goals I have for my children. Little by little, as they mature, I will release to them a certain level of leadership along with its responsibilities. I'll never call it back. By the time they have reached a certain level of maturity (not age, remember, *maturity*), I'm going to put in writing their own, individual declaration of independence. I want to show them ultimately and officially that they are on their own.

Aside from a phone call, a handshake, or contact from time to time—which would thrill me to death—they're on their own to raise their lives before God. I'm there and I'm available, but I'm no longer their head.

Think about that. When you give *yourself* away, also give your children away so they're not left wondering, "Where do I stand?" Let them know they're on their own. Encourage them in it. It will help take away this so-called sorrow about "losing your children." And you'll be gaining—and the world with you will gain—a responsible, purposeful citizen.

Don't Plan For The Pasture

The third reminder for growing older and better is *adapt willingly*. Read to verse 3:

If the clouds are full, they pour out rain upon the earth; and whether a tree falls toward the south or toward the north, wherever the tree falls, there it lies.

Solomon is showing us the inevitabilities of life. Clouds will pour out rain, trees will fall. He then gives us a word of counsel:

He who watches the wind will not sow and he who looks at the clouds will not reap (v. 4).

If the clouds come by, full of rain, it's going to rain. When the tree is cut down, it's going to fall and stay there. If you occupy yourself with the inevitables, the obvious, the ultimates, that's all you'll amount to—just an inevitable, obvious person who ultimately dies. You won't even sow and you certainly won't reap.

When you adapt willingly, you make plans to accomplish something. An older man who had just retired was asked by a young friend, "What are your plans, now that you're re-tiring?"

"Well, my first year I'm going to buy a rocking chair and put it on the front porch," sighed the older gentleman.

178 "Oh, that's great. What are you going to do the second year?"

"I'm going to rock in it."

Hey, listen to me! Sitting in a rocking chair and rocking away one's life is like watching the clouds rain and a tree fall. All that stuff is obvious. Inevitable. It's not sowing and not reaping. When I think of retirement, I think, "Wow, that's your chance! You're free to put it all together!" You're unencumbered. God has given you enough time to really seek accomplishments—if you're ready and willing . . . to adapt.

Don't think older people are merely headed for the pasture. Four major poets who lived to be over eighty years of age did more work in the last decade of their lives than they did between ages twenty and thirty. William Gladstone took up a new language when he was seventy, and at eighty-three he became the Prime Minister of Great Britain—for the fourth time. At eighty-three! Alfred Lord Tennyson wrote *Crossing the Bar* when he was eighty. John Wesley was eighty-eight and still preaching daily with eminent success, eloquent power, and undiminished popularity. At eighty-eight! Every day! Michelangelo painted his world-famous *The Last Judgment* when he was sixty-six.

Had enough? Listen to these comments from J. Oswald Sanders as he writes about having a Caleb-like mentality:

> *The late Canon C. H. Nash who founded the Melbourne Bible Institute and trained a thousand young men and women for Christian service, retired from his principalship at the age of seventy. At eighty, he received assurance from the Lord that a further fruitful ministry of ten years lay ahead of him. This assurance was abundantly fulfilled. During those years he was uniquely blessed in a ministry of Bible teachng to key groups of clergy and laymen—probably the most fruitful years of his life. When he was nearly ninety, the author found him completing the reading of volume six of Toynbee's monumental history as a mental exercise. . . .*
> *Mr. Benjamin Ririe retired as a missionary of the China Inland Mission when he reached the age of*

seventy. When he was 80 he decided to learn New Testament Greek. . . .

(Greek! When I tackled Greek, I was in my twenties and had my hands full!)

. . . he became proficient in reading the Greek New Testament [in his eighties!]. At ninety, he attended a refresher course in New Testament Greek in a . . . seminary. When he was a hundred years old, he was present at a meeting at which the author was speaking. In his pocket was a small well-worn Greek lexicon which he used to brush up his Greek while travelling by public transport![7]

And to think that some people believe that retirement means "I'm finished." The Bible is full of illustrations of how those who are older are to teach the younger ones.

But in order to do that we *must* break out of any rut! Adapt willingly where you are right now. Old age is tough, but when you consider the alternative, it isn't *that* tough!

Trust God: He Makes No Mistakes

The fourth reminder is *trust fearlessly.*

Just as you do not know the path of the wind and how bones are formed in the womb of the pregnant woman, so you do not know the activity of God who makes all things (v. 5).

You don't know the path of the wind and you don't know God's plan. So He says:

Sow your seed in the morning, and do not be idle in the evening, for you do not know whether morning or evening sowing will succeed, or whether both of them alike will be good (v. 6).

Here's a tender touch with reality. Solomon is saying, "Hitch your life to the only security there is, and that is the living, moving, active God." Nothing will keep a life younger than being in touch with the mainstream of God's activity. And that includes enduring loss as well as enjoying gain.

I appreciated what Catherine Marshall wrote following the death of her godly and dear husband, Peter. Prematurely

180 stricken with a fatal heart attack (he was only forty-seven),
Peter Marshall was shaping Congress and moving Washington D.C. as no man has done since then. Suddenly, he was
gone. In describing how she overcame her grief, she said she
finally became absolutely convinced that being lost in grief
can become nothing more than a selfish act of self-pity. It's
saying in effect, "I don't believe in a sovereign God. I don't
accept the fact that He took my mate." When she realized that,
she turned her efforts to writing. And who hasn't been blessed
by Catherine Marshall's pen?

What is the alternative? To just sit alone and live alone?
Solomon says, "Sow your seed in the morning and don't be
idle in the evening." Like the old hymn says:

> Sowing in the morning, sowing seeds of kindness,
> Sowing in the noontide and the dewy eve;
> Waiting for the harvest, and the time of reaping,
> We shall come rejoicing, bringing in the sheaves.

Look at the second stanza:

> Sowing in the sunshine, sowing in the shadows,
> Fearing neither clouds nor winter's chilling breeze;
> By and by the harvest and the labor ended,
> We shall come rejoicing, bringing in the sheaves.[8]

Ever wonder what that meant? It means reaping the benefits
of a fruitful life. Planting now, sowing now, being confident
that God will raise it up later for something for His glory.

My grandfather is a living memory to me. That dear man
was a household word in the little town where he lived and put
in his strokes as judge and justice of the peace. L. O. Lundy
was the byword for integrity. For some reason, God chose to
take his dear wife, my mother's mother, at age sixty-three,
much earlier than He took him. My granddaddy just took a
notch in his belt and started in. One of the things he did was
to build into my life. I'll never forget it. The times we were out
fishing in the bay or the times in his home, he put his arm
around me and just shared his life and the things he had
learned. He just decided to pour it into me.

When my wife and I got married and we needed some financial help for our first home, guess who came to our aid? My

granddaddy. I paid it back slowly but surely, and he never once reminded me of the debt. Faithfully, he stood by me. Little did he know the importance of the investment of his life in mine. He could have become a lonely recluse, locked himself in his huge home, and died early in self-pity. But he believed in a sovereign God who makes no mistakes.

I know a woman in Houston who once stood at her husband's grave, grieving. She suddenly realized, "There's no life here. Why are so many of us weeping over the tombstones." She determined before God, "This will be my ministry." She became a "cemetery evangelist," visiting with people who kept returning to that place trying to talk to the dead. Her vital faith in Christ led her to share Him with hundreds who grieved. That's her ministry. She may be getting older—but she's better than ever!

You're Never Too Old To Rejoice

There is one more principle for growing old, in verse 7, *rejoice daily.*

The light is pleasant, and it is good for the eyes
to see the sun.

That means it is good to still be alive. It's good to be able to look up and see the sun, even though it may be blurred. Verse 8 adds:

Indeed, if a man should live many years,
let him rejoice in them all. . . .

There it is—rejoice daily! If you can't think of something to rejoice over, manufacture it. Ask God for it.

The other day I said to my wife, "Honey, I hope I never get too old to enjoy life."

She said, "You won't, honey, you won't."

The greatest delight of my life is just living—preaching, writing, laughing, studying, investing in my family's lives and in others' lives. It's a delight to stay young and be engaged in the lives of others.

The worst thing I could do—with all that I have gained through life—would be to carve out a cave and crawl into it, to wait until I die. There's too much going on outside to do that!

182   These guidelines will keep that from happening. Write them down and review them regularly:

Live realistically.
Give generously.
Adapt willingly.
Trust fearlessly.
Rejoice daily.

Take this prescription twice daily and, who knows, you may live to be a hundred.

And every year, you'll get better.

[1] Dag Hammarskjold, *Markings* (New York: Alfred A. Knopf, Inc., 1978), p. 6.

[2] Alex Haley, *Roots* (Garden City, New York: Doubleday & Company, Inc., 1976), p. 357.

[3] *"The Reigning Victorians,"* in *Home* magazine, *Los Angeles Times*, 13 May 1979, pp. 14-20.

[4] Wayne Dehoney, *Homemade Happiness*, J. Allen Petersen, ed. (Wheaton, Illinois: Tyndale House Publishers, 1971), p. 402.

[5] "The House With Nobody in It" by Joyce Kilmer, copyright 1914 by George H. Doran Company from the book POEMS, ESSAYS AND LETTERS. Reprinted by permission of Doubleday & Company, Inc.

[6] Charlie W. Shedd, *Promises to Peter* (Waco, Texas: Word Books, 1970), pp. 21-31.

[7] J. Oswald Sanders, *Robust in Faith* (Chicago: Moody Press, 1965), pp. 87-88.

[8] Knowles Shaw, "Bringing In the Sheaves," *Triumphant Service Songs* (Chicago: The Rodeheaver Company, 1934), p. 139.

WHAT TO DO WITH AN EMPTY NEST

Of all God's creatures on earth, humans have the toughest time with an empty nest. Mama bears seem to have no struggle at all saying good-bye to their cubs then going on their merry way. Dogs suffer no depression as their pups bound away to make their homes elsewhere. The same is true for horses with their colts, rabbits with their bunnies, and eagles with their eaglets. But humans? That's another story entirely.

Five Stages In A Marriage

Marriages pass through progressive cycles, each one having its own unique set of challenges. Lofton Hudson suggests there are five distinct stages:

1. Family founding. From the wedding until the first child is born.

2. Childbearing. From the birth of the first child until the first child enters school.

3. Child rearing. From the first child entering school until that child begins college and/or leaves home.

4. Child launching. From the time the first child leaves until the last child leaves.

184   5. Empty nest. When the parents are alone until the death of one of the mates.[1]

It's the fifth stage I want us to think about briefly in this final chapter. For sure, there are pressures and demands connected with the first four stages—sometimes making it almost too difficult to continue. There are, however, many more other subtle hazards that threaten a marriage as the nest empties.

Some Empty-Nest Adjustment

It doesn't take great brilliance to name the problems of this stage in a marriage. Let me suggest several.

Decreasing Physical Attractiveness

Physically, we begin to show our age. We start to sag and slump! Erma Bombeck said it best when she admitted, "I've got everything I had twenty-five years ago. But now it's all four inches lower."

This plays psychological havoc with a marriage in these years. It affects our self-esteem, our sexual drive, our compatibility, and our feeling of oneness with our mate.

Increasing Selfishness

Hard as it is for us to admit, the empty nest is often occupied by two very stubborn, self-willed people. Chronic nagging and criticism can increase. Indifference toward people and life in general also tends to grow as does irritation in accepting the unpleasant and the inconvenient in life. Few, indeed, are the older couples who happily adapt to the changes that impact their lives.

Boredom and Depression

Because of a number of factors, an empty nest can turn into a grim existence: unemployment, retirement with little money and no plans, sickness, fears, and the death of dreams in life. Who hasn't ached over aged parents who become trapped in this boring, depressing syndrome!

My own father lost the joy and light of his life when my mother died in 1971. She had been his spark, his motivation for living. Not being a "people person," he leaned on her for those delightful evenings with friends, those musical interludes each week, those fun times of conversation, laughter, trips, and visits with others. Her sudden departure left him 185 stunned. Immobilized. Alone, in the truest sense of the word. Although we, his children, later cared for him and reached out to him, he soon became a man of boredom and occasional depression—a sad tragedy that often brought us to tears.

Loneliness

I did not mention this with the previous group because loneliness is, perhaps, the single most commonly mentioned difficulty of an empty nest. It needs to be considered by itself.

Busy, active children are gone. Car pools, ball games, piano recitals, school stuff, and everything from going on a date to selecting a mate are past. And rare is the marriage that stays healthy as it endures the vacuum created by all those things screeching to a halt. This is *especially* so if the husband-wife relationship needs the parent-child relationship(s) to keep it strong. Or if one of the parents found more fulfillment in one of the children than in the marriage partner.

Another factor in loneliness we dare not overlook is widowhood. The pain of death is frequently increased because the living mate is left with only a small insurance policy and a mortgaged home. The kids are married and gone, friends and relatives are busy, and life quietly caves in, bringing that uninvited guest to every meal—loneliness.

Retirement

Although I mentioned this earlier, retirement brings its own unique adjustments that deserve special mention.

Retirement can be delightful or devastating . . . a dream come true or a dreadful nightmare. It all depends on how one prepares for it. If it "just happens," watch out! Many a marriage partner puts everything in neutral and rapidly loses touch with life. Like the attitude in a little poem you may have read:

I get up each morning, dust off my wits,
Pick up the paper and read the obits.
If my name is missing, I know I'm not dead,
So I eat a good breakfast and go back to bed.[2]

186   Right now that sounds like a super schedule to me! But I cannot imagine living like that on a regular basis with my wife and keeping our marriage strong. No, retirement often reveals just how much creativity we have . . . or how *little*. Being workaholics by nature, many American couples would be blown away if retirement suddenly occurred.

Divorce

A growing group of people in today's generation is the large body of divorced individuals. They live with another kind of empty nest—an absent mate. This adds to the frustration of rearing children—a demanding job even for partners! Single parents struggle with very distinct experiences unlike those in any other type of family.

In recent years our church in Fullerton finally decided to ignore the single parents in our fellowship no longer. Under the very wise and capable leadership of one of my associates, Ken Bemis, we formed an organization called Single Parents Fellowship. I figured we may have fifty or sixty, maximum . . . but I was wrong. We have *hundreds* who now meet together on a regular basis. For worship. In small groups. To pray. To love and support one another. To share their anguish and struggles as well as their joys and pleasures.

It's booming! The benefits for having such a ministry far outweigh the difficulties. I would encourage other churches to do the same. Believe me, the divorced people in churches today are usually the loneliest, most misunderstood, most-often overlooked people in the flock.

These are just a few of the challenges that accompany the empty nest. Now let's turn our attention to some biblical counsel on what to do, how to cope—and even *enjoy*—the afternoon years of a marriage.

Solomon Speaks Again

Remember the Scripture we dug into so deeply at the beginning of this book? Can you recall the section out of Solomon's writings in Proverbs? In case you have forgotten it was Proverbs 24:3-4:

By wisdom a house is built,
And by understanding it is established;

And by knowledge the rooms are filled
With all precious and pleasant riches.

Remember that famous "Swindoll amplified paraphrase"? It went something like this:

> *By means of wisdom (that is, the skill of seeing things with discernment) a house can be remodeled into a home that attains to a flourishing condition—*

> *By means of understanding (that is, the ability to be sensitive and keenly aware, responding positively to others) that home can be set in order . . . made right—*

> *And by means of knowledge (that is, a teachable spirit that allows room for true facts to emerge) each individual area will overflow with valuable, worthwhile treasures (like memories and relationships) which will endure anything that comes.*

With that in mind as our goal, let me share with you some closing thoughts on what to do as you see your nest emptying or, perhaps, as you stand *today* surrounded by the reality of an absent mate or grown children who have left the nest. I promise to be concise and clear.

Three Practical Suggestions

Drawing these thoughts from the Proverbs passage, let's emphasize the three major terms by way of application.

Exercise Wisdom

We learned that wisdom really means seeing with discernment. Like God does. Having *His* perspective. Looking on life as *He* looks on it. Such perspective will bring an enormous load of encouragement and objectivity.

But how? You're asking that in your mind, aren't you? Well, start by renewing your devotion to the Lord. If you are the superdependent type, you have been (in days past) all wrapped up in your mate or your kids. Almost totally. Losing one or both has thrown you into an emotional and spiritual tailspin. Small wonder you have become increasingly more lonely and immersed in self-pity.

188   Look up! Set a watch upon your heart. Begin meeting with the Lord at a particular time each day. That's right, *daily*. Get your Bible off the shelf and get back into it! Establish those vertical priorities that lead to a godly mentality. Refuse to let your feelings dominate and paralyze you.

One further thought: As you cultivate prayer, ask the Father for some specific assistance in keeping a divine viewpoint rather than strictly a human one. Ask for things like:

- Being freed from worry and fear (name some)
- The release of *your* will as opposed to His
- Ability to flex, accept, change, and shift
- Removal of self-pity
- Some ideas on how to be useful to others
- A healthy, active sense of humor
- Proper response to disappointments and loss

Seeing life with divine discernment is not a natural thing, it's *super*natural. But it is attainable, according to James 1:5:

> *But if any of you lacks wisdom, let him ask of God, who gives to all men generously and without reproach, and it will be given to him.*

And it brings such rich fruit. Read James 3:17:

> *But the wisdom from above is first pure, then peaceable, gentle, reasonable, full of mercy and good fruits, unwavering, without hypocrisy.*

Employ Understanding

Looking on life through God's lenses will arouse within you an enlarged capacity for sensitivity. Rather than just getting older, you will begin to see and think deeper, respond better, and react sooner (and much more positively) to circumstances.

Wisdom leads to understanding. Let it happen! Since the empty nest stage usually provides you with more time, take advantage of it. You can become a person of such sensitivity, others will desire your presence. But in order for that to happen, you'll need to have the same prayer on your lips as this one:

*"Lord, thou knowest better than I know that
I am growing older, will some day be old,*

*Keep me from getting talkative, and particularly from
the fatal habit of thinking I must say something on
every subject and every occasion.*

*Release me from craving to try to straighten out
everybody's affairs.*

*Make me thoughtful, but not moody, helpful but not
bossy. With my vast store of wisdom it seems a pity
not to use it all, but thou knowest, Lord, that I want
a few friends at the end of life.*

*Keep my mind free from the recital of endless details,
give me wings to get to the point.*

*Seal my lips on my aches and pains. They are
increasing and my love of rehearsing them is becoming
sweeter as the years go by.*

*I ask for grace enough to listen to the tales of others'
pains. Help me endure them patiently.*

*Teach me the glorious lesson that occasionally it is
possible that I may be mistaken.*

*Keep me reasonably sweet; I do not want to be a saint;
some are hard to live with, but a sour old person is one
of the crowning works of the devil.*

*Help me to exact all possible fun out of life.
There are so many funny things around us and
I don't want to miss any of them."* [3]

                                                    —Anonymous

You see, understanding includes accepting and admitting
our own tendencies yet trusting God to make us bigger, better
people.

Apply Knowledge

Since God promises that the "rooms" of our
marriage and home will be filled with valuable riches by
means of knowledge, we need to take Him at His Word. As we
learned earlier, the knowledge God honors and uses is
applied knowledge. That kind is best demonstrated in a
teachable, open, and nondefensive spirit. The kind that is
always learning, forever reaching, probing, and discovering.

190   One of the most winsome traits to be found among older couples is this desire to learn and then apply that knowledge.

I teach the Bible. That's my bag. As a result I often find myself with my Bible open in front of congregations (none is better than the Fullerton flock!) as well as other groups. Periodically, I encounter couples who have reared their children and emptied the nest . . . and they somehow get hooked on learning the Scriptures. *Talk about fun!* I don't know who enjoys it more, they or I. And the best part of it all is that they genuinely care about putting into use what they discover in God's Word. And by the way, those couples seem to stay perpetually young. It's magnetic!

Well, that's it. Plain and simple . . . one, two, three. Easy to remember, and it works!

Exercise wisdom.
Employ understanding.
Apply knowledge.

In our fine church here in California, we have a delightful older couple whose lives have been anything but easy. Both have lost former mates by death and neither has known an easy life. Had they chosen to focus on their past, they could certainly have shriveled up into narrow-minded, bitter, critical victims of self-pity. But they didn't. No way.

They found each other through a beautiful chain of events. They fell in love and decided to marry. It was marvelous! He was seventy-three, and she was seventy. You have never met two more involved, alive, alert, and positive people their age. Cynthia and I have been in their home on several occasions for dinner (with a roomful of others every time) and had the time of our lives. Their guestbook is half full of names before many months of any new year have passed. A steady flow of people is encouraged and ministered to because Klon and Christine Matthews refused to think, "We're finished. Our lives are over and done with." They are still on the cutting edge of life. I'm convinced neither one will ever stop until death finally overtakes them. They are an incredible pair!

That's the way to handle an empty nest. That's the way it is 191
when God is given full freedom to step in, rebuild, and renew a
drab house into a delightful home. He can do it and He *will* do
it—empty nest and all.

[1] J. Allan Petersen, ed., *The Marriage Affair* (Wheaton, Illinois: Tyndale House Publishers, 1971), p. 401.

[2] J. Allan Petersen, p. 416.

[3] J. Allan Petersen, p. 420.

13

CONCLUSION

Two things have occurred since I started this book months ago. First, I have aged several years. *Whew!* It's one thing to think, "I believe I'll write a book on marriage" . . . and it's another thing entirely to get the thing finished and into the hands of the publisher. I smiled recently when I read Jim Dobson's words as he quoted Sir Winston Churchill's comments on writing a book:

> *Writing a book is an adventure. To begin with, it is a toy and an amusement. Then it becomes a mistress, then it becomes a master, then it becomes a tyrant. The last phase is that just as you are about to be reconciled to your servitude, you kill the monster and fling him about to the public.*[1]

I certainly can identify with that!

Second, our home has returned to a place of calmness and beauty. The remodeling process is just about complete. The drywall dust is gone. The plumbing is done. The tile is installed. The painting is complete. The carpet and flooring are in. The workmen have left. And I am sitting in a study surrounded by lovely oak bookshelves, brown-and-blue wallpaper, plenty of light. Outside the window is a winding brick

194   walkway that is now finished. The front yard is still a mess, however. When the rains end we'll tackle that job. There are still a few places needing attention (there always *will* be), but for the most part, the place I call home now looks like it. The original design is now a beautiful reality.

God knew I needed a real, live illustration of just how much work is involved in remodeling. I thought it would be bad. But bad isn't the word for it. It was horrible!

But it's over. Praises be, it's over! I ask myself as I walk from room to room and as I write the last check to the contractor, "Was it worth it?" While I was in the middle of the mess, believe me, I would have paid somebody to take this place off my hands. But no longer. I'm glad we stuck it out. Yes, it was worth it all.

There's an old proverb Cynthia and I now understand and appreciate more than ever.

Desire accomplished is sweet to the soul.

What we've endured in our house, you may be enduring in your marriage. Some of you are at the hardest part. You'd do anything to get out. You'd happily pay someone to take the thing off your hands. For whatever it's worth, don't. Please don't. God will honor your commitment as you determine to stick it out . . . to work through it. Take it from me, looking back in the years to come, you will be glad you did.

I can think of only one project that has been more difficult than remodeling our home . . . and that has been the remodeling of our marriage. I am honest when I say that of the two, getting a marriage together is far more uncomfortable, more costly, more time-consuming, and more demanding than getting a house in shape.

But it is also much more rewarding. The "sweetness of the soul" that comes from God's rekindling and preserving a marriage cannot be compared to any other accomplishment on the face of the earth. But unless the project is undertaken, something that was once beautiful and delightful will fade and fail.

Some time ago a very talented young lady wrote a poem at my request. I told her about this book I was writing and then asked that she create on paper the scene of marriage in need of attention. Perhaps her words describe where you are coming from.

I especially appreciated what she wrote because she described something she had had to imagine in her head. She is not married—yet. She will be, however. She is my future daughter-in-law, Deborah Jean Morris. I'm convinced you will read more of her work in the years to come:

>*In those days*
>*the words, "I love you, honey,"*
>*were said with fifty different inflections*
>*and meant fifty different things.*
>
>*They could have meant*
>*thank you for opening the catsup bottle,*
>*even though you said that I had loosened it first.*
>
>*Or I enjoy our talks*
>*when you come home from work*
>*and there's just the two of us to share and dream.*
>
>*Or simply that I appreciate all those things*
>*that make up you;*
>*your sensitive strength,*
>*the way you smile me off my soapbox,*
>*or the way that you pretend you are listening*
>*when you read the paper.*
>
>*But somewhere along the way we turned*
>*and instead of floating with the current,*
>*we now struggle against it.*
>
>*It wasn't one action, or one word,*
>*but a series of little unresolved spats and quarrels*
>*that now make the TV the solution*
>*to the problems of a hard day*
>*and silences us when we should say*
>*"Thank you" or "You really look nice today."*
>
>*Today, I no longer tell you that I love you*
>*because the sound of those words*
>*mocks the special meaning that they carried*
>*when we were first wed,*
>*and it is too painful to remember*

196

that those feelings we said we would never lose
were, tear by tear, left in the past.[2]

How true. How terribly true! Not just one action or one word. Not a single little isolated incident once or twice a year . . . not huge chunks pulling loose, causing sudden devastation. No, not that. But rather a subtle, almost unnoticed wearing away . . . a series of little yet consistent cracks, ever widening and silently ignored. It happens every day of every year all around this globe of hurting humanity. It is a universal problem in marriages . . . *but it is not inevitable.*

And that is why I have written this book.

I long to communicate to every couple I can possibly reach that the living Lord has designed a way to make it work. He holds out hope and encouragement—a divine blueprint for marital restoration. And because He is the Originator of the plans, I can declare (without reservation) they are workable, reliable, believable, and attainable. And best of all, He promises His strong arms of support and assistance to all who determine to return to His inerrant Word and trust Him through the painful yet essential process of change.

Are you willing?

Will you trust Him in spite of your seemingly impossible situation?

Please do! He anxiously awaits this opportunity to strike the original match in *your* marriage as you allow Him the room He needs to rekindle and preserve the flame that once was there.

---

[1] Dr. James Dobson, *What Wives Wish Their Husbands Knew About Women* (Wheaton, Illinois: Tyndale House Publishers, Inc., 1975), p. 177.

[2] Deborah Jean Morris (unpublished poem, March 2, 1980).